D1605612

What a Life

How the Vietnam War Affected One Marine

Semper Fi

By
Randy Kington

Randy

PUBLISH AMERICA

PublishAmerica

Baltimore

Second printing

ISBN: 1-4137-0326-7
PUBLISHED BY PUBLISHAMERICA, LLLP
www.publishamerica.com
Baltimore

Printed in the United States of America

Dedication

I dedicate this book to the many Marine brothers who shared their lives with me, to God who saved my life and soul, and to my wife Patty, who sacrificed her life so that mine would be complete.

Acknowledgments

I am indebted to so many people for helping with the form and content of this story. My parents' and grandparents' patience come to mind quickly. Thanks for believing in the Scripture that indicates if one raises a child in the right way, eventually the child will become what his parents and God wanted him to be. My gratitude goes to Dr. Victoria Barker for correcting my many grammatical errors and encouraging me to complete the story. My good friends, Joe Owen, who wrote about his experiences at the Chosin Resevoir in *Colder than Hell*; Carol Brewer and my uncle, Lamar Black, gave me many good pointers and much encouragement. I especially owe a debt of gratitude to fellow Marines Ted Gray, Ray Wyatt, John Hollars, Ed Brummett, Tom Hood, John Boren, TC Gardner, Chester Gafkowski, General Gary Brown, and retired Commandant P.X. Kelley for their many suggestions.

Table of Contents

Foreword

I first met Randy Kington in September 1965 when he reported to the Rifle Platoon I was fortunate enough to lead for 11 months in Vietnam. Randy was a transfer from the Seventh Marine Regiment, which had fought beside our Regiment, the Fourth Marines, on "Operation Starlite" the previous month. "Starlite" was the first major combat action by US Forces in the Vietnam War. Our Battalion, the Second, was known as the Magnificent Bastards and had deployed as a unit from Hawaii in March 1965 as one of the three infantry battalions of the First Marine Brigade. Our ties were close and our small units were cohesive because of our prewar training together. Incoming transfers with different arrival dates than our original Hawaii (Pineapple) Marines were common at that stage of the war; otherwise, Marines in units such as ours would have all "rotated" back to the States at the same time rendering the unit combat ineffective.

Newcomers were looked upon with some reservation in a unit whose Marines had been together for such a relatively long period. The Seventh Marines' transfers were, however, treated as brother Marines, especially since they had been bloodied alongside us on "Starlite." I noticed immediately that Randy had an inner strength that was more intense than the average young 18-year-old Marine in the platoon. I was impressed by his good cheer and constant smile in the face of the worst of adversities. I also noticed that the other Marines showed him deference because of his natural leadership ability.

Soon after Randy arrived, the Platoon Radio Operator was transferred and the position needed to be filled. This is a critical billet in a Rifle Platoon because maintaining communications with higher headquarters is a must. This is the Platoon's lifeline where requests for air and artillery support and medical evacuations originate. Good communications can make the difference between life and death for every Marine in the platoon. There is also a very close bond that naturally develops between a platoon commander and his radio operator. Randy was the best I had ever seen and I was soon very dependent on his operator skills and could rest assured that he would always be close by when needed. He was an extraordinary Marine in all respects.

Randy's arrival and accession to the radio operator billet coincided with a change in the sea state of the Vietnam War. "Starlite" signaled the change from random guerrilla encounters to combat with Main Force Vietcong Units and North Vietnamese Army Regulars. Randy tells this story in his book with a compassion and understanding that brings the story to life and the individual Marines become real people in the reader's mind. His accurate and poignant descriptions of combat action are laced with insight into his fellow Marines and their challenges and triumphs in the face of danger and adversity.

This book in its entirety tells the story of a remarkable Marine and human being. The chronicle moves from his high school days through boot camp to the Seventh Marines and to Third Platoon, Company "E", Second Battalion, Fourth Marines, and to the fateful day on 21 March 1966 - "Operation Texas." This was an intense encounter with North Vietnamese Regulars that was described in Second Battalion history as the most intense combat to date in Vietnam. Both Randy and I were wounded on that day. I escaped with a minor injury but Randy's wounds left him paralyzed from the chest down and in a wheelchair the remainder of his life. This action is related in illuminating detail on the pages of this book.

An even more remarkable story is that of Randy's recovery from his debilitating wound, devotion to Jesus Christ, building a family, and his business success - all gained from his wheelchair in the years following "Operation Texas." I did not learn of this story until April 2002, when we met in a restaurant in Ellington, Florida, 36 years after we were wounded and separated. There is a great lady who was also at that meeting, his wife Patty. Her devotion and constant support was a most significant factor in the success told in this remarkable story. He has confided in me on many occasions since our renewed friendship how much she meant to him during the difficult years after "Texas" when he was rebuilding his life and future.

There is no bitterness. He is as proud as ever to be a Marine and to have had the opportunity to serve his Country in combat. He is the essence of our belief that "Once a Marine, always a Marine."

The story in this book is testimony to the indomitable courage and determination of the great American that is Randy Kington. It is men like Lance Corporal Randy Kington, United States Marine Corps, who made our Nation great. We can all thank God for him and men like him, who will ensure for generations to come that America will remain a land of free men with unlimited opportunity.

I have taken the liberty of including on the following page the summary of the award recommendation I wrote, which describes Randy's heroic action during "Operation Texas." As you will see, humility is another of the many positive traits that define his character. May God continue to bless America with men of his caliber.

Gary Brown
Brigadier General
U. S. Marine Corps (Retired)
21 March 2003
Saint Petersburg, Florida

LANCE CORPORAL JOHN R. KINGTON
UNITED STATES MARINE CORPS
(MEDICALLY RETIRED)

"For heroic achievement in connection with combat operations while serving as a Platoon Radio Operator with Company E, Second Battalion, Fourth Marines in action against Communist North Vietnamese forces in the Republic of Vietnam. On 21 March 1966, during "Operation Texas," Lance Corporal Kington's Company was designated as the assault unit against one of the most heavily fortified hostile villages encountered in Vietnam to that date. When his platoon had approached to within fifty meters of the objective, the enemy unleashed a heavy volume of fire on the Marines, wounding several in the initial burst. Reacting instantly and disregarding his personal safety, Lance Corporal Kington's first action was to move to an exposed location that permitted him to transmit the platoon situation to higher headquarters. Fearlessly braving the incoming fire, he moved from position to position with his Platoon Commander and assisted him in directing his men's fire on the enemy by giving clear and cogent instructions on the radio. As another platoon was moving into position adjacent to Lance Corporal Kington's unit, both its Platoon Commander and Platoon Sergeant were seriously wounded and disabled. Lance Corporal Kington's Platoon Headquarters then assumed command of the adjacent platoon. Displaying exceptional acumen and initiative, Lance Corporal Kington was able to effectively gain communications with both platoon's squads by radio. This was accomplished in the midst of hostile fire while the Marines were consolidating their hastily established defensive positions. Facing a quickly deteriorating situation, Lance Corporal Kington moved to a relatively exposed position on top of the dyke with his Platoon Commander to gain a clear view of the battle area to facilitate transmitting requests for air and artillery support together with the urgency of ensuring that all casualties were clear of the strike area. Shortly after arrival at this position, Lance Corporal Kington's Platoon Commander was wounded by one of two enemy soldiers emerging from concealed positions. With complete disregard for his safety, Lance Corporal Kington courageously exposed himself, killing one enemy soldier by rifle fire, and sustained a wound in the spinal cord from the second enemy in the process. Although in intense pain, with his arms and legs paralyzed, Lance Corporal Kington heroically remained with a replacement radio operator ensuring his relief was properly briefed and in possession of essential cryptographic codes. Only after the tide of the battle had shifted in the Marines' favor, did he allow himself to be evacuated for treatment of his wounds. By his exceptional courage, presence of mind in a dire emergency and unfaltering dedication to duty throughout, Lance Corporal Kington served to inspire all who were involved in the engagement and upheld the highest traditions of the United States Naval Service."

Introduction

The first day of spring 1966, began as a comfortably warm and deceivingly quiet morning. The sky was a big bright blue that seemed to have no ceiling. I was a six-foot-two, 190-pound, nineteen-year-old platoon radio operator serving with the Second Battalion, Fourth Marines in the Republic of South Vietnam. That morning, after a long helo flight from Chu Lai, my battalion landed in an open field about one thousand yards west of an uneventful looking village in the Vin Tuy valley. From the air, the village appeared to be a beautiful oasis of jungle greenery and thatched huts surrounded by a vast sea of green rice paddies. The village, 90% of which was underground, just happened to be headquarters to a Regiment of North Vietnam's finest soldiers. As we were exiting the hatch of the hurried helicopter, it never dawned on us that this place would soon turn into a horrible killing field — for them and for us.

Lieutenant Gary Brown yelled, "Move it out!"

We slowly but methodically stormed toward the ditch line. Moments earlier, Marine Skyhawks had dropped their deadly cargo of napalm on the heavily fortified trench line. We figured as a result of the huge napalm fireball, all of its occupants would be burned to a crisp.

Our platoon had advanced approximately fifteen feet when one of the low-flying helicopter pilots radioed the command post, "Colonel, my God, they are coming out of the holes, huts, trenches, and tunnels! There are hundreds of them everywhere!"

It was too late to stop us and let the artillery soften up the target. Echo

Company was in front of the battalion as the lead assault group. We had 157 men and would face maybe 1500 of North Vietnam's best in a matter of seconds.

March 21, 1966, was the defining day of my life. Who I was before and who I have come to be after that day is the story of this book. For thirty-six years, I subconsciously blacked out my time in the Marine Corps and Vietnam. I was always proud to have served my country, but I rarely ever talked about it. Maybe it was all the negatives over the years that many people piled on about Vietnam. Irrationally, I think I felt guilty that I was unable to do my job on March 21, 1966, when Lt. Brown and my fellow Marines needed me the most.

On April 6, 2002, Brigadier General Gary Brown, USMC, Retired, and I met for the first time since March 21, 1966. The General hugged me and told me he loved me. Our meeting was akin to a religious experience for me; I felt that everything was now okay. Almost immediately afterward, the memories started to flow and I wanted to share them with anyone who would listen.

Gary suggested that I write down some of my remembrances about the time we had spent together in South Vietnam. This began as a compilation of memories for my children and grandchildren to know who I was then and am today. After finishing it, I decided that the book was also about the men who served with me. I hope that the telling of these memories allows others to know a little of what the Marines were facing in 1965-1966 in Vietnam. This story was written after many discussions with other Marines and from my own memory. I have cleaned up the language and have changed some of the names to protect the guilty.

July 31, 2002, was a renewing of old friendships. It is true that once a Marine, always a Marine. A dozen or so members of Echo Company, Second Battalion, Fourth Marines who served together in 1965-1966, were reunited in Savannah, Georgia. There is probably not a closer brotherhood than that which is bonded under fire. The United States Marine Corps, the greatest fighting force this world has ever known, will forever be a part of me. After all of these years, I still have the greatest respect for the men who served with me and feel that the word Marine should always be capitalized when referring to them.

For some the Vietnam War was hell on earth, for me it was my chance to escape from hell.

Chapter One
"Odds In Our Favor"

On December 5, 1965, a helicopter went down about twenty miles south of the Marine Air Base at Chu Lai. I don't remember if it was shot down, or just had engine problems. The pilot and co-pilot, who both were later rescued, crashed landed their Huey in the courtyard of an old French fort. The compound had a real moat around one-third of its outside wall. The fort straddled Highway One and inside its walls was a white plank-board Catholic church with a tall bell tower steeple.

According to our executive officer, First Lieutenant William Van Zanten, the fort garrisoned a large group of local South Vietnamese soldiers called Popular Forces (PFs), but the pilot reported the place to be strangely empty. Because there were no reports of recent fighting in the vicinity, higher ups were puzzled as to the Good Guys' whereabouts. Echo Company was dispatched to find out what was wrong. The second part of our mission was to guard the crippled helicopter until a big Chinook could fly out the next morning and bring it back to the air base.

The flight from Chu Lai seemed to take forever. We were first landed close to Quang Ngai City and waited for a reconnaissance flight over the area around the downed helicopter. Sergeant Ed Brummett and a squad flew with the recon helicopters and, after scouting the surrounding area, were to secure a landing zone (LZ) for the rest of us.

About three miles from the fort, Brummett radioed to Battalion Headquarters and transmitted, "Colonel Fisher, there are Viet Cong all over the place!"

The pilot chimed in, "He's right, Colonel, they are everywhere!"

Lt. Col. "Bull" Fisher told Brummett to land close to the fort and he would radio the rest of the company and have them down there pronto. Ed's chopper finally set down in a rice field about a mile to the west of the fort and formed a circumference perimeter of about seventy-five yards.

It was late afternoon by the time Echo started to land. As each chopper unloaded its human cargo, the perimeter of Marines thickened around the LZ. With half of the company in place, Captain Jerry Ledin dispatched two Marines to scout and enter the walled hamlet, and then radio back any findings, ASAP!

PFC Tom (Top Cat) Gardner reported back that the fort was deserted. He said, "We entered through the huge gates and climbed the stairs to the second floor of the gate house. We thought we saw VC jumping out of the windows. When we looked out the openings, we didn't see anything."

The company had been dispatched out with Vietnamese interpreters and two long-distantce radios, maybe ten times more powerful than the one I was carrying. We were so far from the airbase that the powerful radios were needed to stay in contact. Headquarters had given us the fort garrison's frequency and, upon landing, we started dialing their number. The PF troops could not be contacted anywhere. There were probably over one hundred members of the South Vietnamese Army stationed there with their families and belongings. It appeared as if they had vanished into thin air.

As soon as the last chopper unloaded its Marines, we formed up and headed toward the fort. We stayed on the dirt road instead of slogging through the rice paddies, which was not standard operating procedure. Charlie was becoming very proficient in mining well-worn paths and roads; however, we were out in the open with little cover.

On the march toward the fortress, many had the feeling that we were being watched. As a matter of fact, the rear of the column was being fired upon continually. The prevailing thought was, if the enemy wanted to fight, they would attack us while we were out in the open. The Company Commander must have been thinking the same way because he really pushed us toward the fort.

We made it inside the huge open gates of the fort, which was identified on the map as Dong Quang, at about 1800 hours. There was absolutely no one inside except the scouts, and that was alarming. Even in openly Viet Cong villages, the enemy always left the elderly, women, and children behind. There weren't even any animals inside. None of us could ever remember being in a populated area where not one barking dog could be found.

The downed chopper was sitting in the middle of the compound. It looked as if no one had touched it since it had landed. Actually, outside of the crumpled, brownish-green sheet metal, the helicopter was as clean as if it had been run through a car wash. We carefully checked the crippled Huey and the surrounding area for mines and booby traps. Everything was found to be in order.

Many of us thought the Vietnamese forces had simply deserted their post, taking their families and possessions with them and the VC had not had time to take advantage of the situation. However, in the back of all of our minds, we thought, *What if Charlie is leading us into a trap?* We were too far from the base to get artillery support. Dark would be in a few minutes and that would probably ground the flyboys and their fighter planes.

Echo Company Captain Jerry Ledin assigned the platoons their areas of responsibility. Third platoon was assigned an area located behind a high, thick bamboo fence. Between the bamboo fence and our foxholes were rolls of stretched-out barbed wire. The place was damp and devoid of any vegetation, which indicated that many people recently had used this area as living quarters. Everything looked very orderly except for the absence of the local inhabitants.

This was my first time out as the Third Platoon's radioman, and I stuck to Lieutenant Gary Brown like a glove. Captain Ledin seemed really nervous. It was obvious he was placing himself in the shoes of a competent Viet Cong leader. If the enemy attacked, where would their leader think the Marines' weakest position to be?

Our weak points were strengthened by the Captain. He double checked each platoon's location and their fields of fire. He was constantly seeing to it that we were ready, alert, and focused. The Captain told us he was going to set up his CP in the church steeple. Even though that was the most dangerous position in the fort, he thought he could better direct a possible attack from the bell tower because of its 360-degree view. I was glad I was not his radio operator that night. To climb up those steeple steps, carrying the heavy PRC 10 radio, would have been tough, but the worst thing would have been to be parked in a such a cramped and exposed position. If I were the VC commander, the moment I saw that long radio antenna flying out of the tower, I'd have used every weapon in my arsenal to destroy the obvious: Echo's Command Post.

Just before the sun went down, Lt Van Zanten noticed some Vietnamese with their rifles held in the air walking our way. The interpreter was sent outside to find out what was going on. His radioman transmitted back that they were remnants of the fort garrison. Van Zanten found out later the South Vietnamese had been attacked by a large force of Viet Cong two days earlier and had fled into the countryside. When they saw the Marines enter the fort, the locals came out of hiding. By dark, many more of the Vietnamese were coming in out of the jungle. The Captain wasn't sure who these people were, so he had them surrender their weapons and stay in the church. Two guards were stationed at the door and were instructed to shoot any of them if they left the building. He didn't want them inside of our perimeter with a weapon, like in the *Trojan Horse*. No one knew for certain if Charlie had or had not infiltrated the group. If these were friendlies, where were their families? Nothing added up.

Lt Brown set up our platoon command post under a big oak tree close to a small interior concrete wall. We all removed our packs, and I started to test my radio with the other operators in the fort. Lt wanted to take the first watch, the platoon staff sergeant the second one, and I would take the next one. I started to remove my boots and crawl in the sleeping bag when Lt Brown advised me that there was a good chance of something happening. He said, "If I were you, I'd keep my boots on just in case." When a Marine officer suggests, one should always consider the suggestion a direct order. I did.

About thirty minutes before sunset, one of our men fired his weapon and yelled, "I got one!" Many ran over to the moat and sure enough there lay a young enemy soldier, lifeless, holding on to a hollowed-out reed that allowed him to breathe under the dark water.

Most of us were thinking, *Was this VC a scout? What information could he tell his boss that could not be had by watching us march in?* They would know our number, the types of weapons we carried, how much ammunition we possessed, and the radio antennas would indicate the range. Could he have been a sapper and was just waiting for dark to fall to do his dastardly deed? We searched the surrounding area for any weapons or satchel charges and found none. It was obvious that this young man gave his life for no reason.

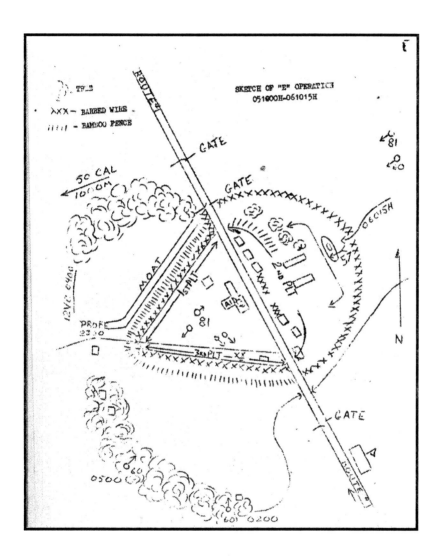

This sketch of the French Fort at Dong Quang was drawn by Captain Jerry Ledin as part of his after action report to the Fourth Marine Regimental Headquarters, dated December 6, 1965.

About two hours after dark, the enemy started probing Third Platoon's front lines. We could see and hear them running to our front. They seemed to be in groups of tens and fifteens. Periodically, a mortar shell would land close by, then our 60 and 81 millimeter mortars would respond. Thirty minutes would pass and then they would fire again and then we would respond again. I don't remember anyone being very alarmed. After all, the tactics the Viet Cong had been using for the past six months usually consisted of firing and then running away. The prevailing thought was there was no way Charlie would ever fight us man to man.

Sometime around 0200 hours, a mortar shell exploded inside our compound. Then another one and another one. Was I glad I had on my boots! We were under attack! They were firing recoilless rifles, mortars, and small arms at us. The battle started in front of our platoon's line but eventually found its way to Second Platoon's area of responsibility. Second Platoon had no formidable barrier to their front like we did. They had only a few strands of concertina wire and a few saw horse barriers to slow down an enemy assault.

Second's Commander, Lt. Fred Williamson, had his men dig in before dark and around 2200 hours moved everyone's foxholes (the Marine terminology is fighting hole) back toward the church about twenty yards.

Sure enough, at approximately 0200, Victor Charlie walked their mortar explosions into the exact same place where the men had originally dug in. Charlie charged the wire and blew holes through it using bangalore torpedoes. They were coming in screaming waves. They were breaking through our lines. Ted Gray's squad fought off the enemy using hand-to-hand tactics. Fighting was so close that Corpsman Ron Isaac was seriously wounded by a VC bayonet stab. Charlie was so close, we could see the flash from their mortars as they were fired. It seemed as if they were firing their tubes almost straight up into the air. We were sitting ducks! Illumination flares were fired that would light up the whole area. The VC melted into the landscape and slowed down on the attack as long as the light was turned on. As soon as dark came again, we would hear bugles blowing and the fight started all over. They probably had done this same thing to the local PFs two nights before and caused chaos.

Everybody seemed to be cool as cucumbers. Our officers and NCOs were out in the open, directing fire and barking orders like this was a training mission. We were taking some injuries and still there seemed to be no panic. Echo's corpsmen were outstanding, risking their lives to attend to the injured

Marines. One of the corpsmen was up on the moat wall and heard a Marine yell, "Corpsman, quick, I've been shot!" He was forty feet in front of the wall and holding on to his foot.

We had called for a helo lift to evacuate some of our wounded. Lt Brown moved a squad out of the fort to secure a landing zone for the med evac to touch down. The yelling Marine was one of those squad members. Doc Martin grabbed his bag and tried to jump past the dark green moat water. He missed and landed in the nasty stuff. He was trying to wade out when something grabbed him. Doc literally flew out of the moat and onto the ground. He found the uninjured Marine. The young man had been shot in the heel of his boot but the round had not penetrated his foot. The heat from the tracer projectile made him think his whole foot was on fire. Doc, who now was wet and coated in foul-smelling algae scum, screamed, "Next time make sure you are shot before hollering for a corpsman!" Even with battle raging all around us, we still couldn't help but laugh at Doc. At first light, Doc Martin looked into the moat and saw a water-bloated Viet Cong soldier floating where he had been grabbed.

We took incoming rounds for most of the night. There were plenty of explosions close to the church. One barrage found the church steeple and did plenty of damage. The Captain and his radio operator were hit with recoilless rifle fire. The operator was mortally wounded. Captain Ledin meanwhile was covered with shrapnel and bloodied, but was still on his feet and in command. The Vietnamese inside the church must have been scared to death, but we kept two guards on them the whole night. No matter what, the Captain was not going to take a chance on allowing the enemy within our walls. We gave much more terror than we received.

I learned quickly why the Captain brought along those big radios. Their operators dialed the Navy who were sitting off shore for some assistance. Also the Air Wing was contacted. They couldn't send up the Phantoms, but did send what they could. A Navy ship sitting about fifteen miles away kept huge rounds flying over into the enemy positions all night. There were planes flying overhead dropping illumination flares. When one would empty his supply, another plane would soon appear with more illumination. I'm still not sure which one was more important to us because the light caused Charlie to be less aggressive. It also showed us where they were. Our men, with their small arms, kept tracer round after round firing into the enemy all night.

All of Echo Company responded magnificently the night of December fifth. As the morning sun rose, we could see Victor C crawling away. Most of us stood on the wall and, like John Wayne, took target practice on the fleeing enemy.

The best quote I heard during my time in Vietnam occurred that night. With explosions all around us, the Captain coolly, and in no hurry, walked over to where Lt Brown and I were. He told us to expect much more action the rest of the night. The Lt wanted to know what size force were we up against.

Captain Ledin calmly and confidently said, "They have about a battalion surrounding us. I think those odds are in our favor."

He didn't smile, he just turned and went out to check on another platoon. Chesty Puller, the most famous Marine of all time, couldn't have said it better. We had 160 men and Captain Jerry Ledin convinced us we were better off than the 700 or so enemy soldiers who had us surrounded! The morning proved the Captain right. We had taken very few casualties, but that particular battalion of Viet Cong was decimated. We only counted seventeen confirmed dead; however, there were bloody marks all over the battlefield where they had pulled bodies off. The seventeen dead had their feet tied together so they could be pulled away easier. In our hurried search of the battlefield, we found meat hooks the VC used to pull their dead away. Now that was a gross sight! We probably killed as many as 150 freedom haters that night and wounded at least twice that many.

Why did those fools attack us? Many attacked standing straight up running toward us. Some of our more experienced NCOs swore the enemy was doped up. Previous battles should have taught them a lesson with all the destruction that we had rained on them. Every day we were becoming more acclimated to the weather and terrain. We were becoming more confident in our own abilities, each other's abilities, and more proficient in killing the enemy. We thought we were some bad men. We knew it, and knew the enemy knew it. The actor, Walter Brennen once said, "No brag, just fact." That was us. A Captain back at Parris Island on November 10, 1964, was right when he said we were members of the greatest fighting organization this world had ever known.

About 0630 hours, a huge helicopter hovered over the crippled Huey. Lines were attached and secured and in no time both choppers were headed toward Chu Lai. Forty-five minutes later, pilots were ferrying us back to our base. On the return trip, I observed that there were no hoorays, no braggadocios bravado, no "I killed a Gook or six Slant Eyes." Actually, an hour after landing, no one said anything about the previous night's fighting, which was named by headquarters as the Battle of Dong Quang.

That was the way it was; after a fight, a long patrol, an all-night ambush, after witnessing a good friend die or be injured, we went on to the next assigned task. Was I becoming jaded or was this the way a Marine was supposed to react? It wasn't that we didn't care, because we did. I believe we simply could not allow ourselves to lose control of our emotions.

After I came home, it took twenty-five years for me to let go and cry. During highly emotional events such as funerals, I could not cry. The one exception was when I heard "Taps" being played. How did I get to the place that my feelings seemed to be so hard? What kind of training would be so thorough that it produced not only hard bodies, but hard minds?

Chapter Two
The Early Years

I was born to Bob and Deola Kington on December 31, 1946, in a small rented white house in a community called Prospect, located just outside of Cleveland, Tennessee. My dad served in the Navy during WWII in both the European and Pacific theaters. He joined the Navy at the young age of seventeen. Grandma Kington had died three years earlier and Granddad was not able to take care of him. He was passed from relative to relative until the Navy offered him a position he couldn't refuse. The service gave Dad a place to call home, discipline, an opportunity to mature, and a vehicle to travel to exotic places like England, Waikiki Beach, and Moscow, Idaho.

After boot camp, Dad was sent to Idaho to learn administrative and radio skills. To an adventure-seeking young man, this was not a very glamorous vocation. Dad had envisioned being a gunner, a navigator, or even a captain of some battleship, but never in a hundred years did he want to spend the war years shuffling papers. The scuttlebutt was if one wasn't happy with his particular school, one could either wet the bed or be a sleepwalker. Dad decided to try sleepwalking. One night about two a.m. he got up and with his arms straight out, started walking up and down the barracks' aisles. Nobody saw him, so he went outside where the patrols were. Whoops, he was barefooted, wearing only his skivvies and there was ten inches of fresh snow on the ground. He turned to open the door and it had locked. Dad "woke up" and, after much pounding, another sailor awoke and opened the door. Dad ran to his bunk shivering and crawled under the blanket. He decided that radio school was not so bad.. Three meals each day, free medical and dental, free clothes, spending money, thirty days vacation, and free education was great, even if it wasn't learning how to shoot down Jap planes.

Dad made the most of his years in the Navy. He returned home to Cleveland and enrolled in Lee College, studying accounting under the GI Bill. My father was a very competent accountant for over fifty years and passed that profession down to my sister Vicki, and me. To think, if someone had noticed Dad sleepwalking that snowy morning in Moscow, the world may have been deprived of three accountants.

Mom was a shy, seventeen-year-old, naive, preacher's daughter when this worldly eighteen-year-old sailor swept her off her feet. They were married September 1, 1943, in Dalton, Georgia, on one of Dad's leaves. Mom worked the two years he was away and when they were reunited, she had saved enough money to furnish their apartment and allow Dad to attend college. Dad was great at managing someone else's money, but he wisely allowed Mom to handle the family funds. When Dad had extra, everybody had extra; he was generous to a fault. Dad was the unquestioned leader of our family, making most of the decisions as to what to do, where and when to go. Mom, however, always controlled the purse strings.

While Mom was shy and satisfied to stay in the background, Dad was just the opposite. He never met a stranger. He loved to get out and go places and do different things. He really enjoyed getting up in front of large groups of people while Mom hated the limelight. He directed the choir at every church we attended. Mom enjoyed a life of home and reading. On her seventy-sixth birthday, she estimated she had read over 12,000 books. Dad became very sick in 1987 and for the next ten years was dependent on my mother to lead. Mom's personality completely changed. She now is outgoing and loves to meet new people. As long as Dad was out front, Mom was happy with her supporting role. When the leadership role was thrust on her, she assumed it with ease.

My first memories of life are of a seventeen-acre wooded spread way out in the country. Dad purchased the rustic property while he was in school. A spring provided us with running water — us running to the spring, dipping a bucket into the water, and running back. When nature called, we used an outdoor privy with a half moon carved into the door. Toilet paper consisted of pages from a Sears and Roebuck catalog. Electricity was laid shortly before we bought the house and land. Mom still cooked on a wood-burning stove and the house was heated by a fireplace in the main room. Both of my parents worked, but found time to plant a large garden. What a great place to grow up — thousands of trees and paths on which to play.

My Aunt Katherine and Uncle Ira kept me on their farm while the folks were working. The farm was a working one with family members doing most of the labor. The hard work was accomplished with mules because they didn't own any mechanized equipment. The most memorable thing that happened at their house was that I saw a naked female for the first time. One of my girl cousins said she would take her clothes off if I would. We did. We were both less than five years old.

I smoked my first cigar at the age of four. We attended a church with an outdoor privy, and I just had to go. Dad was directing the choir, and Mom let a teenage boy take me outside. After the visit, he and I went over to where some guys were smoking. One of the boys asked jokingly if I wanted a puff. "You bet," I said and grabbed his cigar. The choir had just finished and Dad walked outside to check on me as I started to puff on the stogie. He came down to where we were and told the guys to watch as he spanked me They begged him to give me another chance, but he said all of us needed to learn a lesson, and we did.

Dad was very impatient. He could never keep a secret. One day after Thanksgiving he said Santa wanted me to try out a gift, and if I liked it, he might bring me one for Christmas. I was nearly five. That Friday, Dad and a family friend opened a box that contained an electric train set. They played with it all afternoon. I only got to watch the adults because if I touched the Lionel locomotive, Santa said it would spoil my surprise on Christmas Day.

In September of 1951, I started to school in a three-room building housing eight grades. The school was called White Oak and sat on about ten acres across from White Oak Baptist Church. The pastor and principal were one and the same. There were five other first graders in Ms. Spurling's first, second, and third grade classroom. Ms. Spurling was my favorite teacher ever. She would pick me up at the bus stop in her brand new Studebaker for a ride to and from school. I was always spending the night at her house. She really showed me a lot of attention and made me feel very special. If all first grade teachers were like Ms Spurling, I believe our young people would be more likely to succeed. Shower a kid with self-confidence and he will be the better for it. I know I was. Twenty-five years later, I tried to be the same kind of teacher as my first grade teacher was for me.

My sister Vicki was born that year and was I in for a rude awakening. I was no longer the center of attention. Competition came from a beautiful little blued-eyed darling, and I didn't like it one bit. I did everything I could to show this intruder I was first and didn't want to share my position. One day "blue eyes" was sleeping and I shook her bed just enough to wake her and cause her to cry. Dad sat me down and pulled off his belt. He assured me the whipping would hurt him much more than me. He was dead wrong. I don't ever remember using that line with my boys. I was always learning lessons the hard way!

In October, 1953, Dad felt the urge to "go West young man" and California here we came. We sold everything except our clothes and loaded the four of us into a creme-colored 1949 Chevrolet Coupe. That small back seat was home to Vicki, box upon box, and me for four days. Everything went wrong. We locked the keys in the car in Arkansas and New Mexico and blew a water pump on the border of Death Valley. The Chevy started heating up at a service station under a big sign that said "Last chance to fill up for 78 miles." It was nine o'clock and the mechanic was walking out the door to go home. He said it would take at least two days to get a '49 pump and we would have to hang around until he could repair it. After seeing our ragged family he said, "Wait a minute. I have a rebuilt 1949 water pump," and installed it that night.

We drove into Ontario, California, that next morning. We spent the next few days at the home of the Whipples, some of Dad's college friends. Soon Dad got a job at the orange juice plant. We rented a four-room bungalow in Upland and enjoyed sunny Southern California for the next twelve months.

In November of 1954, Dad decided that Tennessee was the place we needed to be. We loaded up the Chevy and eastward we went. Vicki and I were bigger, and yet there was room for our new television along with everything else in the back seat. Our destination was Morristown, Tennessee, where my grandparents pastored a church. Dad intended to get a job quickly and move us into our own house.

After a few days in Morristown, my father became seriously ill. There was no money or insurance to see a doctor. Dad kept getting sicker and weaker. Christmas passed with him continuing to go down hill. I remember hearing someone say, "Bob is so sick he may die." I went upstairs and knelt outside his door and asked God to make my dad well. Many more people were doing the same. A few weeks went by and Dad started to recover. Soon he was out looking for a job.

We later moved into our own house. The neighborhood kids were Hanky,

Footney, Sister, and Brother. Vickie and I were the only kids there with normal names. Fairmont Street was a strange place, and we fit in just fine.

The winter of 1954, I learned a lot about my grandparents. They housed us, fed us, even bought me school clothes and supplies. That Christmas, Vicki and I received as good a Christmas as their three kids who were still at home. They never complained. Looking back, my grandparents' example before me likely contributed to my surviving March 21, 1966. My granddad was smart, athletic, strong, and could excel at anything he put his mind to. He chose to serve God in full-time ministry. At his funeral we learned hundreds had accepted Christ as a result of Reverend John Black.

I was the first grandchild and was made to feel very special. My grandparents were the type that made me want to excel and do the right thing. When I did do wrong, they were the last people I wanted to find out. It wasn't that they would punish me or not let me forget the wrong, it was that I had let two wonderful people down. One of my most special letters in Vietnam was from Daddy Black. He wrote, "Don't get killed, boy." The way he expressed the statement I knew he would be hurt very badly if I did not make it back. He was a strong-willed, uncompromising, but very diplomatic, problem-solving, loving preacher.

I was probably ten when Dad really got after me for something Vicki had done. She was always getting me in trouble. I devised a method of payback. Dad always got out of bed and would walk into the kitchen and get a drink after he thought we were asleep. He would never turn on the lights because he would be in just his shorts.

As soon as everyone was in bed, I crawled into the kitchen and placed ten tacks in a way that led to the sink. I waited for one hour and sure enough I heard Dad put his feet on the floor. Revenge was at hand. After a few steps the sounds, "Ouch! Oh, oh, dang, crap, Oh, Oh," came from the kitchen. Seven out of ten was not bad. I got tickled and could not stop laughing. I could have gotten away with the payback if I could have just controlled my emotions.

The first nine grades, I never attended the same school two years in a row. We were either moving or the school board changed the bus routes. I was constantly saying goodbye to old friends and making new ones. I was always starting over. Sometimes that was good, but not always. At each new school there seemed to always be somebody who, for a variety of reasons, didn't want me there. I was tall and must have had that "please beat me up" look because I was getting into a lot of fights during the fall of each new year.

At Alpha School in the sixth grade, a popular athlete decided he didn't like the new kid. The teacher left the room and he came over and pushed me. I pushed back and soon we were down on the floor wrestling all over the classroom. Somebody shouted that Mr. Heisler was coming back. We made a date to finish fighting the next morning before class.

All that evening and night I kept thinking, *What have I gotten myself into now?* All of the other boys hung with and looked up to this kid and were rooting for him to whip me. I was truly dreading getting off that bus the next morning as it pulled onto the school ground. Half the school was waiting next to the well house where the big event would take place. I was about to be beaten and humiliated in front of all those girls, and worse, hurt. I knew I had to do something before I got hurt badly. Instead of you push me, I push you, I lit into that kid's face with one fist after another. He fell back and then down. I landed on top of him and flailed away. Finally he asked for relief, and I was awfully glad to accommodate him. After that fight it seemed as if I had a "reputation." Don't pick on the new kid, he picks back. That kid and I became good friends, and neither one of us ever mentioned the fight at the well house.

I got a paper route the summer of 1960, delivering *The Knoxville Journal*. The route only had sixteen customers to begin with and had to be delivered around five o'clock in the morning. My pay was less than two dollars per week, but only if everybody paid. I doubled the customer base to thirty-two and won a four-day, all-expenses-paid trip to Washington D.C. Besides all the familiar sights such as Arlington and the Smithsonian, the highlight of the trip was attending a Senators verses Yankees baseball game. Roger Maris and Mickey Mantle each hit home runs. What a thrill! That fall I took on another route and brought home almost nine dollars a week.

I drank my first beer at the age of thirteen. I had an appointment at an optometrist's office in Knoxville. Two friends laid out of school and rode a Trailways bus the forty-five miles with me. After the visit we had three hours to kill before the next bus to Morristown. One of us suggested we buy a six pack of beer. I was elected to do the purchasing because I looked the oldest. There was no problem with the clerk and off to the river bank we went with a six pack of bottled Miller. I opened my bottle and took one swallow and almost puked. I remember saying it tasted worse than spinach juice. I refused to drink any more of it, even when my friends questioned my manhood. Heck, if it took drinking this awful stuff, I wasn't so sure I wanted to be a man.

High school was special. Coach Salisbury wanted me to play football, but I was used to all the extras my earnings were providing. I wasn't a very good player in junior high, but regret not giving high school football a chance. I had swapped my paper route for a career in retail sales — a bagboy at George's Market, and later, the A&P store. The extra money was used to buy the kind of things the popular kids had. Our family had a new addition, little sister Terri, and Mom and Dad were strapped for money. Mom was now unable to work and Dad brought in all the family funds. It was a great help with me buying my clothes, and providing for my school expenses.

I think earning my own money from age thirteen taught me lessons that have lasted over forty years. Responsibility and money management are just a few of those lessons. Many school extracurricular activities were missed because of work; however, the benefits seemed to far outweigh the cost. I have second guessed myself many times about the way I raised our two sons. I encouraged both to play sports and participate in as many school activities as possible and wait until they were grown before going to work. I probably deprived them of some very valuable life lessons.

There were plenty of negatives to having extra money at an irresponsible age. I was able to smoke (60% of our high school boys smoked), drink, go places I shouldn't, and do mainly what I wanted. Independence in my case caused me to be to a disobedient son who thought he knew more than he really did. Maybe the memory of all those rotten things I did influenced my discouragement of Johnny and Josh from starting work early.

Trouble was my teenage middle name. I probably skipped school an average of at least once a week. Staying out late was commonplace. I believe I hold the record for most paddlings in a school year at Morristown High School. Whenever something wrong happened, I was always the first one called to the office to be interrogated. I was usually guilty. One time, though, I was accused of letting the air out of a teacher's tires and I was innocent! The sophomore English teacher SAW me commit the crime. The assistant principal, Jack Pemberton, confronted me with his "eye witness" evidence.

Mr. Pemberton was at least 6-2 and weighed about 225 lbs. and had already given me some of the hardest paddlings I had ever had. His hero was Alabama football coach Paul "Bear" Bryant. He put a lot of effort into being a tough disciplinarian like the Bear. He said, "Bend over."

I don't know where I got the courage, but I said, "No, I didn't go near her car yesterday." The truth was, I had skipped school that afternoon and clocked in at work early. If I told where I really was, I would have had to bend over anyway.

He was startled. "Let me call your parents," he said.

Mom answered the phone, and after hearing the evidence against me said, "If I were you I'd give him more than a paddling."

He hung up and said, "Come over here, now!"

I said, "I promise, I am innocent this one time, Mr. Pemberton." For some reason he believed me. Whew!! I was so mean my own mother didn't believe me.

My sophomore year I bought a 1955 baby blue '88 Oldsmobile coupe for $495. My folks cosigned a note with me. The payment was $25 monthly, and most months it was an ordeal to scrape up that much cash. I was crazy about that car, but it seemed to hate me. Weeks after buying it, the transmission died. I found a used one for $15, but the labor wiped me out. The motor mounts had to be replaced. A battery, alternator, gaskets, tires; that thing was draining me dry. It was parked or "out of order" most of the time. I still was crazy over "Baby Blue."

I met a young lady who had the look of "if you take me out you'll get lucky." I had parked Baby Blue for a few weeks because I didn't have the money to purchase the license plate sticker. Solution: the sticker was green in 1963, just like Green Stamps...

I picked her up and off to the drive-in movie we went. This gal had on at least one pound of make up, lipstick, and eye stuff. She wore the loudest perfume I had ever smelled. She asked if we were going to stop at the Big Top Drive-in for a Coke before the movie began. My first mistake that night was pulling in to the drive-in and turning off my engine. After all, I only got four and a half miles per gallon and one hundred miles on a quart of oil. Baby Blue wouldn't start. I tried everything. I was so embarrassed, and worse, I had spent a lot of money and no drive-in. That rotten car had to be hauled in to John Brock's service station.

Dad just happened to be returning home when he spotted my car. I don't ever remember him being so mad. "What are you doing out driving without plates, and who is that woman?" He ordered me into his car and I got in.

"Can we take Marcia home?"

He never answered. One of the guys at the station took her home. It took months for me to live down that fiasco.

I was visiting with my best friend Johnny Talley one night. I backed out of his driveway with Johnny outside of the car guiding me. We both observed the new neighborhood girl across the street looking our way. Johnny said,

"Burn some rubber," and walked behind the car. I tromped the pedal to the floor and almost killed him! I didn't realize I was still in reverse. Johnny wasn't hurt badly, but the worse thing was the fool I had made of myself in front of the new girl.

Baby Blue was constantly causing me grief. Patty Wilson and I were driving on a back street when we got stuck. We were both wearing nice clothes, so I called John Brock to haul us out of the mud. The next day Patty's brother and I were at the station when John said, "Jackie, you should have seen this dish Randy was out parking with last night."

Jackie looked at me and said, "You were out with my sister!"

John quickly retracted his statement. I spent days trying to convince Jackie of the truth that nothing happened.

My sixteenth summer, I got a construction job helping build a large nylon plant outside the city. Eighteen was the minimum age, so I picked up some dirt and rubbed it into my sophomore hands. The guys coming out of the office said they were looking at hands. It worked and I became a construction worker. What an exhausting three months! I ran a motorized dirt tamper for sixty to seventy hours a week with no days off. I really didn't want to be off since overtime paid $1.87 per hour. I paid my car loan down that summer, but that was the only positive thing I did. There was a party every night or at least something going on. Even though I still hated the taste of alcohol, I seemed to spend a lot of money on beer. All the people I wanted to be with drank, so I did. When school started back in the fall all I had to show for eleven weeks of back-breaking work was $175 paid on the Olds.

My last year in high school was more of the same trouble. I was on schedule to graduate in three years by taking senior English and Health in summer school. I thought I was pretty smart. My hard courses were behind me except English, and I was looking to breeze through. One of the easiest courses left was World Geography. The summer after the third grade, Dad bought a set of World Book Encyclopedias. Reading about places like Asia, America, and Europe was awesome. I memorized the capitals, populations, rivers, mountains, islands, and historical things such as wars, generals, presidents, and such.

World Geography was after lunch and I was always sleepy. Mrs. Roark, who taught the course, was one of my former paper route customers, and I was sure she would cut me plenty of slack. I sat in the middle of the class and fell asleep during her first lecture. I woke up as the class was taking a pop quiz. I aced the test, and she thought I had cheated. I kept falling asleep because I was so tired from working, staying out late, and the course was so easy. I didn't have to study to do well, and she was sure I was cheating. She started watching me very closely and would often search my desk and books. It became a game. I would bring a suspicious paper to a major test. Mrs. Roark was sure it was a cheat sheet. Mid-way through the test she would run to my desk and jerk the suspicious paper out, only to learn it was blank. She wanted to catch me cheating so badly, but I really didn't have to cheat.

With three weeks of school left, Mrs. Roark was discussing the Iberian Peninsula. She pointed out that only two countries shared the area, Spain and Portugal. I interrupted and said, "That's wrong, there are three." I was told to participate only when I had something constructive to add.

That afternoon I copied a report on Andorra, a small republic in the Pyrenees Mountains above Spain. Next day in class I gave her the report and proved that I was correct in front of the class. What a stupid, disrespectful thing for me to do to that nice lady. About thirty minutes later I spoke out of turn and was asked to leave the room. I was expelled from World Geography, the easiest course I had, and would not graduate! She just knew I was cheating and this was her way to distribute justice.

I hated not being able to walk across the stage and receive a diploma, but should have been just as sorry I was so disrespectful. After I came home from Vietnam, Mrs. Roark visited and brought me a pecan pie. She told me how sorry she was that she had dismissed me. I told her it was all my fault and I wanted to apologize to her for being such a wise guy.

In early May, Terry Cranford and I decided to join the Marine Corps together. Two recruiting sergeants visited my parents to convince them this was a good move for me. I needed their permission since I was only seventeen. Mom was dead set against it. Dad, though, said the Navy turned his life around and the Marines could do the same for me. Additionally, the Marines would pay for me to go to college just like the Navy did for him.

Mom said, "What if there is a war and something happens to you?"

"This is the Atomic age; if there is ever a war we all will be blown up," I pleaded.

Mom reluctantly signed on the dotted line. We were sworn in on May 7, 1964, but didn't have to report until September 2, giving me time to finish summer school. Now summer school was down the drain, and I would enter the Corps without a diploma.

My last summer as a civilian was not a good one. I got my old construction job back, but on the application I forgot what day I gave as my birthday the previous summer. Four days later I was fired for not being eighteen. I sold my car, cashed in a coin collection from the paper route days, and worked some odd jobs to support myself. I wanted to get in as much living as possible before Parris Island. Drinking, partying, and getting into trouble was a nightly occurrence. I still hated the taste of anything alcoholic, but I wore a steady path to our local bootlegger's house (Morristown was a dry city).

I was really looking forward to being a Marine. It would be so much easier having a good friend there with me. Terry and I would be together for at least the first five months. Then Murphy's Law popped up its ugly head. A bunch of us were out one night when somebody shouted a fight was starting in the A&P parking lot. Dale Black was about to fight James Roy Peoples. We arrived as James Roy ran to his car and pulled out a gun.

I said, "Terry, let's get over out of the way."

He said, "Naw, I'm a brave…" and was shot mille-inches below his heart before he could finish the sentence.

After weeks in the hospital, Terry recovered, but not well enough to enter the Corps. Now I was facing one of the toughest obstacles of my life, and I would have to do it alone. What a disastrous life those first seventeen years had been.

On the night before I started my service career, Dad and I had a "last supper" of country ham at Harris Motor Court in Bean Station, which was about ten miles from home. On the way, a friend rolled his dump truck right in front of us. *Was this a bad omen?* I wondered.

The next morning we said our goodbyes and it was off to Knoxville to meet the other recruits I would be traveling with. I met a kid named Mike Mclaughlin whose dad taught at the University of Tennessee. Mike and I became good friends and were stationed together for the next eight months.

We boarded a plane for Savannah, Georgia, by way of Atlanta. This was my first time flying and I was apprehensive, but after a few minutes into the trip, I concluded flying was the only way to travel. I picked up a paper in the airport and read it on the flight. The headline was, "Sergeant York Dies." Pall Mall's famous WWI Medal of Honor winner's picture didn't look anything like Gary Cooper.

All of these bad omens, I thought. *What have I done?* I was seventeen, all alone, and looking back, considered my life to be a total failure. I had let so many people down, my grandparents, my mom and dad, teachers, friends, God, and how about me? How could one make so many mistakes in such a short period of time? When did I become this person that even I didn't like?

When did I decide I knew more than I really did? I was selfish, thinking only about Randy Kington, not realizing how badly I was hurting others. What a life these seventeen years had been.

Chapter Three
Transformation

From Savannah the Marines transported us onto the Marine Corps Recruit Depot at approximately 0115 hours. From now on time would be reported differently. No longer would it be fifteen after one, am; now time would be measured by dividing the day into twenty-four hours starting at midnight. Time reporting was not the only thing that would change. I found out years later, from former recruits, that the Corps intentionally brought everyone in after dark so we would believe the only way off the island was to swim across a shark-infested strait dividing Parris Island and Beaufort, South Carolina. I know that's what I believed.

The bus stopped in front of an old brick building which was built in the thirties. The building was known as the recruit barracks and was a holding place until we could be assigned to a platoon. A sharply dressed Marine herded us into the barracks and told us to bunk down for the night. Someone would pick us up the next morning with our assignments. I slept on a red-painted concrete floor until 0600 hours. Little did I realize that 0600 would be the beginning of the most grueling training that I would ever experience. On September 3, 1964, I was a country bumpkin whose life would change over the next eleven weeks from a boy to a man.

Staff Sergeant Gutherie greeted us with expletives that were fighting words back in Tennessee. There was no urge to defend our honor against this man — Sgt. Gutherie was a man among men. He was a highly decorated Korean

War veteran and would be delighted to demonstrate on us how he killed so many Chinese. We lined up with our feet at a forty-five degree angle, thumbs along the seams of our trousers (never call them pants), stomach in, chin up, and eyes straight ahead. He called out eighty-two names and informed us we were now members of Platoon 182.

Drill Instructor Sgt. Gutherie then shouted out for the high school graduates to form a line to his left and the "dummies" to line up on the right. I had on my class ring and thought, *Should I raise my hand and explain that I almost graduated? Should I go into detail and tell about the Iberian Peninsula? Maybe all I need to say was a misunderstanding had taken place and I really had the intelligence to get a diploma. What if I line up on the left with the graduates and if I am corrected, pretend I didn't understand his command?* Dummy is exactly what he called me and that is what I was. I moved in line to the right.

The next thirty minutes were spent with the three Drill Instructors (DIs) introducing themselves to us. Staff Sergeant Gutherie was the leader, and his two aides were Sergeant Bowers and Corporal Terry. Each took time to remind us how horribly awful each one of us were. We were never to look into their eyes. They were to be always addressed as "sirs." We were not Marines until they said we were. For now we were maggot, scuzbucket recruits and would probably never make it off Parris Island. Corporal Terry was the smallest at 125 pounds but the most combative of the three. He ranted and raved and begged one of us to step out and meet him behind the barracks. All eighty-two of us were duly frightened. Sergeant Bowers was from Maryville, Tennessee, about fifty-five miles from Morristown and I hoped he would be approachable since both of us were Tennesseans. I was wrong. It turned out that Terry and Bowers were the bad guys and Gutherie was the good guy. I thought, *I am over six feet tall and weigh 172 pounds. I am not used to anyone talking this way to me. Nobody should call me the names they have.* I was sure it would get worse. It had only been thirty minutes.

The platoon quickly learned commands such as attention, forward, to the left, right, and halt. We were then marched over to the Supply Depot. There we were issued utilities (olive-colored shirts and trousers), socks, tee shirts, boots, and shoes. Everything that was issued was stuffed into a sea bag. Next came the Armory where M-14 rifles were assigned to us. All morning long was spent outfitting us with stuff that would separate us from civilian life. The time was also used to acclimate us to the most verbal abuse imaginable. Shouting and screaming at us for no apparent reason was a nervous breakdown in the making. Pushups and running were the punishments of choice. I probably was the most abused that morning. I kept looking at Terry's eyes when I spoke, and I called him a "guy" and "you." This was definitely the wrong way to start out a new profession.

At about 1100 hours we were introduced to our home for the next eleven weeks. In front of the barracks was the largest parking lot I had ever seen. There were no stripes on the asphalt, and it was referred to as a parade deck. The barracks was a white, two-storied building built during World War II or before. Platoon 182 had the top floor. Austere was an understatement. The steps and hand rails going up were old and rickety. Forty-two double bunks lined the walls and in the middle was a Warm Morning coal stove, sitting on an old wooden floor. Off to the right was the "head" (bathroom) which was built for fifteen or twenty, not eighty-two human beings. We put our gear away and learned to make up a bunk the Marine Corps way.

Twelve hundred hours saw us march to the mess hall. Funny names — do I want to relieve myself in a room called a head, or do I want to eat in a place with the name mess in it? I had never eaten in a non-school cafeteria. I picked up the tray and loaded it up with some good-looking salads. When I got to the meat and potatoes there wasn't room on the tray. I don't ever remember being as hungry as I was after lunch, and I would have to make it until supper on rabbit food. Maybe even worse was the fact we had to eat at attention with absolutely no talking.

After lunch the screaming, yelling, pushing, and kicking started all over again. I lost my hair and had an ID photo taken, in that order. We were then issued personal gear such as soap, shaving stuff, tooth paste, writing paper, etc. Medical and dental exams followed. In the medical department was a Morristown boy, Navy corpsman Jimmy Wilson, Patty's older brother. I hoped Jackie had not shared with him about the night his sister and I got stuck in the mud. I definitely did not need another enemy on Parris Island. At each stop we would stand at attention under the hot September sun while part of the group was inside the various buildings. If anyone fouled up, like not standing straight enough, grinning, or looking at the DI, they were rewarded by doing pushups on the hot asphalt.

Supper was at 1730 hours, and I was starved to death, especially after all of those pushups. I was proud of myself for being such a quick learner. Only one salad this time with plenty of room for meat loaf, mashed potatoes, beans, and bread. That was the best meal I could ever remember eating even though we could not speak and had to look straight ahead.

Getting shots from the Navy Corpsmen was one of the easier things I did at Parris Island.

One Eighty-Two was then marched back to our upstairs barracks for some well-deserved rest — WRONG!! More screaming and abuse amid instructions on how to do things like polish boots and shoes, shave, and clean rifles the Marine Corps way. At 2030 we were told to write home and tell the folks how well our first day in the Corps had gone. Afterward, we had to finish storing all the gear we had accumulated and had thirty minutes to clean up and shower.

At 2200, I finally was able to actually lie down. Lights were turned out and I looked around to see if anyone was looking. I had big tears in my eyes and was about to cry out loud. This was the worst day of my life. Those DIs hated me, I thought, even more than the other guys. This was the deepest mess that I had ever been in and there was no hope of fixing it. I was so scared and alone that I pulled the pillow over my face and cried out loud. I was so glad that the guys back home couldn't witness that scene. What a disaster I had made of my life.

The first week was a blur of doing things a different way and getting acclimated to being away from home. The day started at 0500 with one of the DIs throwing a garbage can down the squad bay, which was another name for the area in the middle of the barracks. I was convinced that crashing sound would have awakened the dead.

The first order of business was to wash down the squad bay floor on our hands and knees with scrub brushes the size of a bar of soap. Next, our racks were made and we dressed. Afterward we went for a nice long run before the sun fully rose. Breakfast was next. When we were allowed to speak in the mess hall, many guys expressed how bad the food was. I thought it was the best food I had ever put in my mouth and there was plenty of it.

We attended many hours of classes on Marine Corps history, hygiene, chain of command, and more. There was at least two to four hours of intensive physical training each day. We were all impressed that the on-duty DI did every exercise with us. To us youngsters, the DIs looked to be in their early fifties, when they were really only in their late twenties to maybe thirty-five. They looked weathered, experienced, worn, and ancient.

Close order drill (marching on the stripeless parking lot) consumed two or three hours each day. It was important because it developed teamwork. Each Drill Instructor had his own style of calling cadence. Sgt Bowers sang his (he was a radio announcer in civilian life). Gutherie introduced ditties like, "You had a good home, but you left, right, left, right…" Terry just screamed. Each day we learned new steps such as column right, oblique left, forty-five angle right, and then we marched doing different moves with our rifles.

One day in the first two weeks, Corporal Terry was screaming and abusing us as we marched. I outweighed this man by at least fifty pounds, but when he got within a mile of me, my knees would shake so badly I thought I would fall on my face. He claimed to be able to stomp any of us in the ground and this seventeen-year-old was convinced one day he would back up that claim — on me!

Terry started walking backwards while calling cadence so he could observe us better. He yelled out, "By the right, hark!"

Quickly my brain asked, *Does he mean my right or his?* I went to his right, while the other eighty-one guys went to their right.

"Platoon halt!" he angrily screamed. "Scuzbucket, maggot, expletive, expletive, Kington, front and center."

I ran over and screamed out, "Scuzbucket Kington reporting as ordered, sir!"

I was at least nine inches taller than Terry. He asked me to bend my head down. I thought, *This fellow is going to whisper some criticism so the other recruits wouldn't hear.* He doubled up his fist and hit me smack on my right ear. The sun was bearing down on us and coupled with the hit, I staggered and should have fallen, but didn't.

Terry then yelled at the top of his voice, "From now on when I say to the right, go toward the ear that hurts, when I say to the left, go toward the ear that don't hurt."

"Aye, aye, sir," I answered and returned quickly to my spot. I never made another marching mistake the rest of the time, so his method of instruction must have worked.

One and a half years later we received some replacements to my company in Vietnam. One of the new guys, Corporal Bingham, introduced himself as a former Drill Instructor sent straight from Parris Island. When asked if he knew a Corporal Terry, he replied, "Yes, we were both sergeants two months ago, but some mama wrote the colonel that we were beating up on her son. We were both busted one rank and I was sent here." What a small world.

Every day I grew up a little more. November 19, 1964, graduation day, seemed a long way off, but September 3 was getting farther behind me. We were constantly having guys drop out and sent back to the beginning. They first spent time in a group called the motivational platoon. When they were properly "motivated," they joined a beginning platoon. That was the worst thing that could happen to us. Death would have been better than losing time earned in boot camp and repeating it. That was the way they were able to maintain discipline and order and get by with intimidating us so easily.

There were no discipline problems in Platoon 182, just some who couldn't do the physical part. Most of those who were sent back were overweight. Everyone really felt sorry for those young men. The worst part of Parris Island was the constant mental abuse. If I told a civilian the abuse these men perpetrated on me, there's no way I would be believed. The physical training was tough enough. Sit-ups, pushups, rope climbing, jumping jacks, one hundred step-ups onto a two-foot-high box, and four-mile runs in heavy boots were only a few of the things we were put through. Everyone gave this training all they had. The constant threat of being sent back was all the motivation it took for us to achieve 100% effort. Whatever it took, I was going to graduate.

Sundays were special. We got to sleep an hour later. The garbage can wasn't used to wake us. Funny thing, most were awake at 0515 but couldn't get up till 0600. Only one DI had duty on the weekends, and he was usually tired of being with us all the time. We were encouraged to go to church and many of us went. Most of the guys weren't being religious; in chapel we could rest and the chaplain spoke softly. We were still required to work and train after service, but Sundays were more bearable.

The platoon pulled Mess (kitchen) duty the fifth week. We were given more freedom because a chief cook was in charge of us. The hours were

Corporal Terry calling cadence for Platoon 182. Terry frightened the daylights out of me.

terrible, the work nasty, but the screaming died down some. I noticed while on the serving line I could tell in what week a recruit was. Those in the first weeks were sloppy and soft. One could see a progression of physiques and confidence with the number of weeks spent in camp. Those in week eleven were confident, strong, and chiseled young men. I was half way to that look, I hoped.

Week six introduced us to more classes such as Judo, hand-to-hand fighting, swimming, tactics, and organization. Three fire teams in a squad, three squads in a platoon, three platoons in a company, companies form a battalion, then regiment, division and then the Marine Corps was drilled into us. The chain of command from President Johnson down to DI Terry was repeated until memorized. We spent hours spit shining shoes and boots. Mine had such a deep shine if I looked down I could see the color of my eyes.

Week seven was more of the same. The verbal abuse never let up. The physical part was getting longer and more difficult, but we were getting stronger, faster, and smarter. One could see the confidence we had in ourselves and each other. One thing was still a killer for us — running in cadence in our heavy boots. I never met a Marine who enjoyed that exercise. The DIs sometimes dropped the bad guy front and talked to us about what to expect in the real Corps. Sergeant Gutherie told us about his war experiences in Korea. I can still see those Chinese charging his machine gun. He killed so many of them, his buddies would have to crawl out front and unstack the piled up Chinks to clear a line of fire. He also told of the platoon lining up to urinate on his gun barrel because it had been fired so much and was red hot and had to be cooled.

We had our first big inspection in week seven. All along, the DIs were putting us through inspections, but this one was to be conducted by the company commander who was a captain. Hours and hours were spent spit shining our shoes and boots. The same for cleaning and oiling the rifles. Ten hours at the minimum were spent hand rubbing linseed oil into the rifle stock. The bunks and lockers were to be in order. We were to line up in front of our bunks, and when the captain smartly turned in front of us, we were to present arms and then do the manual of arms. He would inspect each man and his rifle and proceed to the next recruit.

The captain handed my rifle back to me and said, "Good." He then paid me a huge compliment, "Did you shave this morning recruit?"

"Yes, sir," I lied. I could not believe he actually saw whiskers. I had wondered why I, who only had a little fuzz, was issued a razor. I was feeling like a real man.

The next two weeks were spent on the rifle range learning how to fire that magnificent piece of steel. We had handled, cleaned and oiled the M-14 so much, all of us could break it down, and reassemble it blindfolded. Actually that was one of the requirements to graduate. We were taught about the nomenclature of the rifle such as the flash suppressor, trigger mechanism, bore, and its 7.62 millimeter rounds. We were ready to exit the classroom and start firing.

I had never fired a rifle. I had fired Johnny Talley's shotgun a few times, but never a rifle. I wasn't totally ignorant, I had watched Chuck Conners on *The Rifleman*. The first lecture we had from the line instructor was, "I hope none of you have ever fired a rifle before. It takes longer to exorcise bad habits than to teach from scratch." That was just what I wanted to hear.

We practiced almost every day, with half of us manning the pit area and marking the targets, and the other half on the firing line. We fired from two hundred, three hundred, and five hundred yards. We were firing lying on our bellies, leaning on one knee, and standing up straight. Each day I was improving. I was squeezing the trigger instead of yanking it. My scores were constantly among the best in the platoon. One day Sergeant Gutherie singled me out to pass on to the platoon what I was doing right. Only three other guys were asked to speak to the platoon. My confidence really grew in those weeks. No longer was I this dumb Tennessee hillbilly. The guys started calling me the Tennessee Sharpshooter and Davy Crockett's grandson. I figured the rifle range was my chance to make PFC. Only eight men would be promoted and one promotion went to the top shooter.

We were treated like human beings on the day and night before qualifying. The screaming and yelling changed into encouragement. We were fed an awesome meal for supper. The DIs even took us to the base movie theater to see *The Sands Of Iwo Jima* staring John Wayne. There was no fire watch, so we all had a sound night's sleep.

The next morning we were at the firing range at 0900 hours. An extra hour's sleep and a big breakfast had all of us in a great mood. The sky was barely cloudy and there was just a little wind. I started out with some good scores, but ended up with 211 out of 250 points. That score was good enough for a medal but not PFC. The DIs were graded on how well the platoon did. They had counted on me being a high scorer, and I had disappointed them. I still don't know where I went wrong. The conditions were nearly perfect. Did my nerves and confidence betray me? If I ever go into combat it won't be a score I'm worried about, it will be the people who depend on me and my own life that may suffer.

We marched back to the parade ground barracks that Sunday afternoon. The next two weeks would be spent bringing everything together and applying what we had learned. There were four hurdles that had to be jumped before we could call ourselves United States Marines. Those were maneuvers at Elliot's Beach, the obstacle course (they actually referred to it as the confidence course), close order drill in front of the base general, and the Regimental Commander's inspection.

Even with my disappointing qualifying score, I was still pleased with myself. I only had two weeks left and nothing was going to foul this up for me I hoped. Sergeant Gutherie had the Sunday duty and ordered us to get our gear squared away for the two hours we had before supper. Only a week earlier I thought I had witnessed this obnoxious kid from New York with his hands in my locker box. He denied it. This Yankee had really irritated me that morning before church. He told a bunch of us we were dumb to believe in a dead man. He thought he was better than Jesus because he was alive. I said to myself, "Let it be, he is not worth a trip back to the beginning and spending an extra nine weeks on this island."

Sergeant Gutherie had left the squad bay, and we were cleaning our gear and placing everything away. Yankee was a big dude around some of the smaller guys, but was a yellow coward with anyone his own size. He was walking through the barracks and "accidentally" stepped on the shoes of a little guy from North Carolina. His name was Moore and he was a good friend of mine. Those shoes had at least twenty-five hours of spit shining and now North Carolina would spend extra hours repairing them.

Not fifteen minutes later, Yankee again stepped on the little guy's shoes. This time Moore came up fast like he wanted to fight, but backed down. Yankee said he was smart for being a coward. That was all I could take. Yankee was between two bunks leaning against an open window. I said, "I'm not a coward, but you are. On the count of three I'm going to break your face."

He said, "I don't have a quarrel with you."

I started counting. At three I hit him and broke his nose and sent him sailing out the second-story window. Two guys grabbed his ankles and pulled him back into the building. He ran to the head, slinging blood all over everything. It dawned on me that I was on my way back to the beginning of boot camp. How could I be so stupid?

Sergeant Guthrie ran into the squad bay to see what all the commotion was. He saw the bloody floor and went into the head. There he saw Yankee trying to stop the bleeding. He came out and demanded to know who broke Yankee's nose. I hesitated for five seconds, knowing if I spoke up I was gone. I had to tell the truth; maybe he would only send me down to the fifth week. I blurted out in a high, breaking voice that, "It was me, sir."

He asked why, and I told him New York had insulted my belief in Jesus Christ by claiming to be better than Him and also I thought he was a thief. I hated to be a snitch but this recruit wasn't worth my honor. Then he wanted to know if I had sucker punched Yankee, that is if I hit him when he wasn't ready. "No, sir, I gave him fair warning." I was trembling all over the place and about to break down in front of my comrades. What if nobody had caught the kid from falling out the window and he died? What a mess I was in. Then the unexpected happened, Sergeant Gutherie reached for my hand and shook it. He said, "I'm glad you did it, now get this mess cleaned up!"

"Aye aye, sir," I thankfully blurted out.

On November 10, the Marine Corps' birthday, I was on fire watch, walking from one end of the squad bay to the other. It was about 2300 hours, and I was startled by the company commander. He barked out a question about why non-commissioned officers and above wore a red stripe down the side of their dress blue trousers. I told him it symbolized the blood spent in storming the Halls of Montezuma. He then said something that I will always remember. "Never forget that you are a member of the greatest fighting organization this world has ever known."

"Yes, sir," I answered. I never felt prouder in my life. Nine more days and I would really be part of the greatest fighting force this world has ever known.

The confidence course test was a breeze for us. We were in the best shape of our lives. The course looked intimidating and impossible to complete. Once involved though, we all made it through just fine. We also did great on maneuvers at Elliot's Beach. Some of the city boys had never spent the night outdoors. The mosquitoes and sand fleas were brutal and the food (World War II c-rations) sucked, but we really had a good time.

Platoon 181 had beaten our score on the rifle range and was one of the four platoons with which we competed. They were the only one ahead of us. Close order drill judging was our last competition. We dressed in our best and marched to the reviewing stand. There was a whole bleacher full of top-ranking officers that may have included Major General Masters, a highly decorated WWII hero who was also the base commander. We marched crisply and mistake free that day. All the moves were executed exactly the way we had practiced over the past eleven weeks. Platoon 182 won the battalion commander's trophy and the DIs couldn't have been more pleased. Two more days and we would be United States Marines, unless...

On November 18, the Regimental Commander's inspection would be our last test. Parris Island either takes pounds off those who are overweight or adds pounds if needed. I added about twenty pounds and most of them were in my chest. We had been fitted by a tailor about five weeks prior and now with the added weight, my uniform was tight. I wondered, do I ask for some alterations or try to get by with a uniform that is snug? In the Marines, one learns quickly not to volunteer or ask too many questions. Bring as little attention to oneself as possible. I made a foolish mistake and kept the tight-fitting uniform.

We were lined up to go outside with the DIs giving us one last going over. Sergeant Gutherie straightened up my shirt and retied my tie. Heck, I had never tied a tie before — 1964 was the year of the clip on. He looked to see if I had shaved. I had, honest. The platoon assembled in front of the administrative building which housed the Colonel's office.

The Colonel was late coming out. It was about 1100 hours and the morning sun was bearing down on us. We were at parade rest, which was not as stiff as attention, but stiff enough. I noticed the tight fit at my arm pits. It was causing my fingers to tingle. The Colonel came out and we snapped to attention. This made my fit even tighter. I could just barely feel my arms. The inspector walked down each line and stopped in front of a recruit, turned sharply and reached for the recruit's rifle. The rifle was at the right side and sharply brought up in front of the chest, the left hand grabbed the upper stock tightly, and then he pushed the bolt open with the right hand. We had practiced this procedure ten thousand times.

I was about the fiftieth to be inspected. The Colonel turned to my front. No one had messed up yet, and I was praying I wouldn't either. I picked up the M-14 and it went flying across the asphalt. My arm by now was sound asleep and I didn't fully realize it. There lay my scratched rifle and the stock with all that linseed rubbing. It looked awful. Sergeant Gutherie who was following the Colonel gave me a look that said, "I'm going to kill you when I get you back to the barracks."

The Colonel was cool and not at all upset. He asked, "What's wrong?"

I told him my arms had gone to sleep.

He told me, "Son, everything will be okay, just step out of rank, shake some life back into those arms, and unbutton your jacket."

After finishing the last inspection he returned to me. I did the routine perfectly. No more tests, I was no longer scuzbucket, maggot, recruit Kington, but now, Private John R. Kington, USMC.

November 19, 1964, was a glorious day. Most of us ate at the club and had cheeseburgers and Cokes for the first time since September 2. The DIs told us how proud they were of us, that we were one of the best platoons they had ever had, and we were one of them now. No longer did we have to call them sir. I had gone from a dumb, backward hillbilly to someone who was really proud. I was in the best shape of my life. I was so gung-ho and brain washed. I knew I could handle anybody or anything that came my way, well maybe not Corporal Terry. He still frightened me. I had just accomplished something that would make me proud for the rest of my life. I surmised, "What a life I have in front of me! What is Morristown, Tennessee, going think about me now? What a life!"

I was watching *Gomer Pyle USMC* on television the other night. At one time that was me. I was so green my DI had to help me get dressed. Corporal Terry had me so bamboozled I didn't know left from right. It has been more than thirty-eight years since those three months on Parris Island. That autumn, I started out as a boy. Sometime before November 19, 1964, I was transformed into a man.

Chapter Four
Fine Tuning

November 20, 1964, all of us newly graduated "boots" boarded a bus for Camp Lejune, North Carolina, for Advanced Infantry Training (AIT). Earlier, the Drill Instructors awakened us with the call, "Marines, rise and shine. The buses will be here in an hour and you need to eat a good breakfast." None of us could believe we were being treated like human beings, but now we were members of the same Marine Corps that included Sergeant Gutherie and the Commandant.

We pulled off the island way before daylight. The ride was uneventful except a stretch outside Charleston, South Carolina. At dawn we crossed a two-lane rickety bridge at least eight hundred feet above the water of Charleston Harbor. The bridge was built high enough for the Navy to sail under. Every time the bus met oncoming traffic, I thought we were going to plunge into the water. That was one of the scariest bridges I have ever crossed. The weather was starting to turn cold. At Parris Island I never wore a coat.

We arrived at the base before noon, and were introduced to the instructors. We were assigned to companies and allowed plenty of time to unpack our sea bags. We were at a place within the Camp Lejune Reservation called Camp Geiger. This base made Parris Island look like a modern twenty-first century installation, which it wasn't. The grounds were mature, overgrown, and the barracks were circa WWI. The head was two hundred feet outside the back door and accommodated three other buildings. The amenities were much better, or accessible rather, with a club, PX, and gym with a bowling alley. We were not allowed to go off base for the four weeks of training; however, good use was made of the club. The first day was an off training day, and we all enjoyed that rest.

All of us thought we understood everything Marine upon finishing boot camp. None of us had a clue. In addition to the regular routine such as physical training, drilling, and inspections, we would be fine tuned into becoming combat ready Marines. Each of us took turns throwing hand grenades, firing thirty and sixty caliber machine guns, and firing a 3.5 rocket launcher at an old tank. We were forever marching to mock battlefields, sometimes ten miles away.

Night maneuvers were favorites of our instructors. One night it was thirty-five degrees and raining. We crawled under barbed wire in the mud with machine guns firing live ammo over us, or so we were told. We got back to the barracks at 0300. Our rifles were so muddy, most of us took them to the shower. The next night the temperature dropped to twenty-two degrees. We were divided into fire teams of four, and using a compass, had to find our way out of the woods. Again we got back home at 0300. I was filthy and it took all the effort I had to wrap a towel around my waist and go outside in the freezing cold to the showers two hundred feet away. That night, with the wind blowing off the Atlantic Ocean, was the most miserable experience, weather wise, of my life. I don't ever remember being so cold!

Two memories of Camp Geiger stand out. One was on a cold, windy, overcast day out in the field. One of the instructors asked if I planned on a career in the Corps. I told him most of my friends were in some warm, comfortable school room about then and that's where I probably should be. He said that I was learning more about life than any college would ever be able to teach. Thirty-eight years later I still agree with him.

The second memory occurred while I was on weekend clean-up duty. I was emptying the waste cans from the company office, and this captain asked me to get some sugar for the office coffee. I walked to the club and "lifted" a jar of sugar off a table and returned. The captain saw the jar and said, "I didn't mean for you to steal for me, but I like your initiative. What's your name?" Two weeks later at graduation that same captain called out my name for promotion to Private First Class. There were 220 of us and only twenty-two were promoted. I remember thinking, *I hope my first promotion wasn't because I stole sugar for the captain!*

Everyone had twenty-one days of leave coming upon completion of AIT, and after fifteen weeks, we were all looking forward to going home. I had not had a hair cut since arriving on November 20. I wanted to look good for the home folks, so I got a trim, leaving hair on top, the morning before I was to leave for home. That afternoon the company sergeant assembled us one last time. In formation we were marched to the barber shop. He said with a grin, "You boys ain't goin' home lookin' sloppy." The barber shaved the remaining hair off the top. On the morning of December 22, 1964, I headed for Morristown, Tennessee…bald!

That twenty-one day leave went by very quickly. I was so proud of myself. Mom and Dad bought a set of dress blues for me for Christmas and I wore them everywhere, to the store, to church, on dates. Friends kept coming by and remarking how good I looked. Dad bought a color tv so I would have something to do at home. I believe I watched *Bonanza* and a few ball games on it. Most of the time I was out running around with old friends. Looking back, I wished that I had not been so inconsiderate and instead spent more time at home with some very understanding people — my parents.

My orders were to report to casual company G on or before January 13, 1965, at Camp Geiger. I was then to report to Camp Pendleton, California, for combat training as travel came available. They actually didn't want us in California until the overseas Marines arrived. These men had spent thirteen months in the Far East and were expected at Pendleton at the completion of their leave time. These "salts" would continue to fine tune us into real Marines.

At Geiger, I was put in charge of a platoon. There were about 250 men and only eight PFCs. We were called on to do all the dirty jobs at camp while awaiting our exodus. All of us had 0311 military occupation designations. This meant we were in the infantry, affectionately known as the grunts or ground pounders. If war came, we were the front line.

I really enjoyed being in charge. It was just what I wanted to do; I loved to yell, "Fall in, attention, left face, forward march." One day a major pulled over and had me stop the platoon. He dressed me down because some guys in the back of the formation were goofing off. One more time and he threatened to replace me. I didn't want that, so I really got on the slackers. I heard one of the guys remark that all this power was going to my head. Shucks, these men were friends with whom I had gone through Parris Island. Authority was great, but the responsibility sucked.

We finally got the word to leave for Cherry Point and catch a commercial flight complete with stewardesses to San Diego. It was a four-hour flight, and the Marine seated next to me was Mike McLaughlin, the same guy I started with in Knoxville. We played gin rummy the whole flight. I had played very little cards before this trip. I noticed the object seemed to be lay your hand down the quickest and catch the opponent with cards in his hand. I kept studying the game and decided to try another approach. I would discard cards I wanted to the middle and keep the cards I didn't need. I tried not to go out quickly; instead, I would seed the kitty and then pick it up. My opponent was usually blocked from going out and I would rack up tons of points. I won sixteen straight hands. I stumbled on to a way to fund my college education, I thought. What a life I had in front of me! Everything was working my way.

We landed in San Diego, and were bussed to Camp Mateo, which was part of Camp Pendleton. The bus took the ocean route that afforded a view of all of those beautiful California girls, beaches, and waves. The feeling I had the first night in Parris Island, when I was so miserable and cried, was way in my past. The Marines were just what I needed. I remember thinking there was no amount of money that would make me return to boot camp, but there was nothing I would take for the experience and feeling of accomplishment I gained in those eleven weeks. I have been fortunate to count many successes in my fifty-six years, and the defining moment for all of them started at Parris Island.

The bus pulled up in front of a barracks that looked like it was designed by the German architect who laid out the bunkers at Normandy. They were unpainted concrete structures with flat roofs. The floors were even concrete. That first night we froze! The concrete held in the cold. There was a coal-burning stove in the middle of the big room, but nobody knew how to start it. Besides, this was Southern California — sun, surf, beaches; who knew the winter nights were cold! The next day the "salts" arrived and they knew how to light the stove.

These Marines who had been overseas were an interesting group. They came in with the most fantastic stories about the Philippines, Hong Kong, Okinawa, and Japan. They had been there, done that, and were going to share their extensive Marine knowledge with the "boots" as they liked to call us. They knew all the short cuts to achieving objectives with "if you use your head you don't have to destroy your back" as their motto. They also knew all the good liberty spots in Southern California.

Two young Second Lieutenants were assigned to our company as platoon commanders. There was Mr. Krulak, whose father was a famous Marine general from WWII and Mr. William Blaha, who was a Naval Academy

Here I am getting ready to go on a long march into the hills of Camp Pendleton. Notice how austere our barracks are.

graduate. Second Lieutenant Blaha was given the assignment to head up my platoon. Both men would have distinguished careers in the Corps. Krulak would become Commandant of the Marine Corps, and Blaha would retire a full colonel.

Mr. Blaha was the most gung-ho Marine I ever met. He believed in the "book" and was no nonsense. We were constantly doing extra drills over and above what the other platoons did. There was a hill (mountain) in front of the barracks called Hill 921. We were forever running up that hill, which was so steep one could touch the ground while standing up. Blaha could run up backwards, but the rest of us went up huffing, puffing, and puking, especially the salts. The salts were soft from their leave time and the long boat trip back to the States. We always, somehow, made it to the top of that monster and then had to find a way down, which was not easy. On long marches, the other platoons were allowed to fill their packs with light weight stuff, while we were weighed down with regulation weight. That extra weight was a killer over ten to twenty miles. Blaha pushed us so hard, but I didn't know of anyone who didn't like him.

In early May 1965, we participated on a large amphibious landing operation called Silver Lance. Our platoon was to climb over the side of a ship into landing ships (LVTs) and attack a beach. We took trucks to San Diego and were about to board a large WWII-era troop ship. Mr. Blaha decided to lecture us before boarding. He barked out, "Gentlemen, for the next four days you are going to be side by side with the Navy. You are the best, smartest, and strongest fighting men ever assembled. These sailors are going to look up to you, envy you, and they know they don't have what it takes to be one of us. If I see or hear of you not upholding the honor of the Corps these shipboard days, you will be escorted to my presence and believe me you don't want that."

Upon his tip toes he shouted, "Remember these sailors are not your equals, leave them alone, don't talk to them, don't goof off, and never do anything that will bring reproach on the Marine Corps."

I heard someone say softly, "This crazy man really believes this stuff."

We marched up the gang plank, then saluted the flag and officer of the day. We were assigned bunks and Mr. Blaha informed us he had officer of the day duties that night. The ship was tied to the dock and wouldn't sail until the next morning. The duty room was a tiny six-by-six foot cubicle with a light bulb hanging on a long cord. Even though we were docked, waves still rocked the ship against the mooring posts. Mr. Blaha had been in the little room for about two hours, watching the light on the end of that cord move back and forth. He turned green and ran to the side of the tied-up ship. We had not even moved out of the harbor and our Naval Academy officer was pea green with sea sickness. We were out about two days when a storm hit us and plenty of the guys got sick. The Lt was very understanding. I can still remember him looking like a ghost and advising us to eat plenty of crackers.

I was with First Marines only two more weeks. The time I spent with Mr. Blaha was a valuable learning experience for me. William Blaha was the type of Marine you wanted leading if war was ever declared. A friend who went to Vietnam with him told of his point man stepping on a mine and losing his legs. He said the Lt was deeply affected by the loss and his personality really softened. He absolutely cared about his men. We all knew why he pushed us so hard. He wanted us to be prepared in case we were ever called on to fight . Thanks to men such as William Blaha, I was prepared.

Liberty in Southern California was awesome. John Boren, a Georgia boy, and I became good friends. He was a good influence on me. He was two years older, very smart, and was a non-drinker. We spent weekends in places like Tijuana, Mexico, Long Beach, Los Angeles, and San Clemente, the future home of Richard Nixon, which was located just outside the base gate. On payday weekends we toured the exotic places, and on the other ones we laid around the beach at San Clemente.

I almost died on one of those outings at the beach. That particular Saturday we were wading in the Pacific Ocean, which was full of beautiful girls in skimpy bathing suits. We desperately wanted to impress those California beauties. I kept going farther out into the water to show off. All of a sudden I couldn't come back to the shore. The famous Pacific undercurrent had me and wouldn't let go. I struggled and swam toward the beach with all my might. I yelled to John who was walking back toward the shore, but he wouldn't turn around. I didn't scream for the life guard because of all the girls around and besides, I was a **US Marine** and we did not do stupid things like go out too far! I began to panic, when all of a sudden, I found a small sandy place and was able to dig in my toes. After another ten minutes of using all of my might, I made it to shore. John said he saw me struggling but thought I was clowning around. Pride is sometimes a dangerous virtue.

On one payday weekend a bunch of us went to Long Beach and found this fantastic amusement park, named The Pike. The centerpiece of the park was a huge roller coaster that went out over the ocean and at the time was supposed to be America's longest and highest. For a quarter we boarded the front car and off it went. Twenty seconds into the ride, the bottom fell out. I shut my eyes tightly and gripped the bar for all I was worth. I have faced death more times than I want to remember, but I was never more afraid than on that ride. We rolled back into the station, I opened my eyes, unlocked, actually pried my fingers from the restraint bar, and got out of the car. I didn't know whether the other guys saw how frightened I was, so I bluffingly asked if anyone wanted to ride again. I thought they might have had the same experience as I had. Not!

John said, "Yeah, let's go again."

Quickly I recovered and begged out because I was getting low on funds. Liar! There was no way that I would board that creature again.

I loved my time in California. The food was plentiful and good. Those who were stationed on Mateo had a good idea why the military budget was so high — food. For breakfast I had two to four eggs, two pancakes, bacon, sausage or ham, gravy, toast or biscuits, a sweet roll, and four cups of milk. Lunch and supper were also just as plentiful. The training was so grueling we were forever hungry.

California was the first duty station where we "boots" had some freedom. We were responsible for managing our own money. Payday was every two weeks, in cash, and for many who had never held a civilian job, the pay was gone the first time off base. I learned years before while carrying papers how to stretch my money. A PFC made $46 every two weeks and somehow I never missed but one available liberty. That one miss was the time a hometown friend of John's flew out for a visit. We met him on a Thursday night at a motel outside the base. That weekend was a ninety-six hour pass weekend and most of our NCOs and officers were off the base. We told Jim he could stay in the barracks with us and save his money. We smuggled him aboard base and found him an empty rack to sleep in.

The next morning, he ate breakfast in the mess hall after we found him a uniform and gave him a crash course on who and how to salute. He spent three days as a Marine and had some tall tales to share with the boys back home. I was just glad we didn't get caught. Aiding and abetting the impersonation of a serviceman was, at the least, a court martial offense.

Sometime around the middle of May, the Seventh Marines needed some men to fill out their regiment. Quite a few of us with the First Marines who had never been overseas were transferred. I was assigned to India company, Third Battalion, Seventh Regiment. The Seventh Marines were the most decorated outfit in the Corps. They were the ones who had destroyed the Chinese at the battle of Chosin. If I had to leave Mateo, this group would be my choice. The regiment was in the process of loading all of its assets on an old WWII aircraft carrier named the *USS Valley Forge*. The official word was, Okinawa was our destination. The unofficial rumor was Vietnam, where the Marine Brigade from Hawaii had just landed.

I was assigned to Staff Sergeant Little's platoon and found myself in a fire team of Corporal Barret, and PFCs Parks and Lance. Barret was a Pennsylvania twenty-two-year-old that only had eleven more months in the Corps. Al Lance was a cool California boy who had his own Harley. Harold

Parks was a black man from Arkansas. Parks was special. I had really lived a sheltered life in Tennessee. I can remember talking to only two black people back home — Chester Jobe who helped me keep my Oldsmobile running and a kid who lived two blocks from my house. That kid's parents became angry when they found out he was playing ball with us. They didn't want him playing with us mean white boys. His parents were smart to deny him because we were mean.

Parks was funny and smart. All his jokes started out with, "This ole mean white man or this little white mama…" Harold was a good athlete and it pushed me to stay up with him. If one were looking for a foxhole mate, Parks would be a good first choice.

It took four days of working day and night to load the *Valley Forge.* We sailed out of San Diego on May 22, 1965, for Okinawa with a stop over in Yokosuka, Japan. It took fifteen days to reach Yokosuka. That ship was so old and creaky, we counted our blessings when we reached land. The mess was old and small with little room for cooler storage. We started on powdered milk and eggs within three days of leaving California. The sleeping quarters were thirty-inch-wide, hard-canvas bunks stacked six high. An overweight Marine would never be able to crawl into one of those tight-fitting beds. The sleeping quarters were claustrophobia in the making. The showers were tiny. The only ones that profited from that trip were sea gulls who flew at the fantail of the ship. They were there to eat the garbage thrown over the back. I couldn't believe it, but they seemed to stay in the air the entire fifteen-day voyage.

The fifteen days at sea gave us new guys plenty of time to learn the ways of this group. We were having inspections, doing physical training, and standing watch in between living and staying out of each other's way. The physical training was dangerous because we did it on the flight deck. Some days the wind would blow so hard and the ship would be moving up and down so much that it was a challenge just to stay on the deck. Watches were from 2000 to 0600 hours and were meant to give us practice staying awake. One night my watch was from 0200 to 0400, and my station included me going out on this side porch that had two one-inch ropes as railings. At that time in the morning it was pitch-black dark in the middle of the Pacific Ocean. I touched one of the flimsy ropes and thought, *If I fall, no one will ever know I am missing until role call. Why am I in harm's way? Do they expect some unsurrendered Japanese sub to fire torpedoes at us? Being a Marine is dangerous even in peacetime. What's it going to be like in a war zone? What a life I'm living.*

On June 6, we finally pulled into Yokosuka. There was one day to visit the land of the rising sun and then we were sailing to the main Ryukan Island of Okinawa. We debarked at White Beach on June 9 and traveled by truck to Camp Schwab which was supposed to be our home for the next thirteen months. Camp Schwab looked just like a college campus. The barracks were like dorm rooms with four to a room. The head and showers were state of the art and gave us plenty of privacy. The mess hall was one of the finest, and the base amenities were some of the best the Corps had to offer. I thought I would just retire on Okinawa; it was so outstanding. As a matter of fact, many Marines did.

Okinawa was great outside the gate also. There was a small village a tenth of a mile from the gate. If you couldn't find what you were looking for there, it probably didn't exist. There had to be at least thirty bars in that small village. I did something real stupid after one of my trips to the village. I wrote two letters, one to my dad and one to Terry Cranford. I described in vivid language and detail what Terry was missing on Okinawa. I then stuffed the addressed envelopes with the wrong letters. Dad got an eyeful.

The other bases on the island had better reputations for taking care of their troops than even Schwab. On Saturday, a group of us caught a bus to the Air Force base at Kadenna. We had heard their mess hall was like a restaurant. Sure enough, we walked in the mess and were greeted by a white-jacket-dressed Okinawan who directed us to a table. He then gave us a menu with plenty of different items to choose from. The food was excellent. We all agreed those flyboys had it made.

The third day on the island, jungle warfare training started. The military had built an authentic duplicate of a Vietnamese village. Many hours were spent attacking and then cleaning out the enemy hut by hut. There were pop-up targets triggered to stand up on our approach and supposedly fire at us. On one particular exercise my fire team was crossing a stream. We were alert and focused and still a pop-up target wiped us out. I couldn't believe it was so easy to be killed. How could one stay alive in the real theater of war when it was so simple to be ambushed? Very soon there would not be a referee to mark us KIA when we stumbled. A bullet or land mine would do the deed.

We also went through some extensive physical training. There were some long marches on the island. India company spent a whole day repelling off steep cliffs. This was a first for me and I really enjoyed the exercise. I had never had a fear of heights and that is probably the reason I liked it so much.

Lastly, swimming was emphasized. There was this swim of four hundred yards in the ocean that almost got me. If you were among the first finishers, you got a big "atta boy" from the officers. I swam about half way when I started cramping. Harold Parks saw what was happening and swam back to me. He stayed with me until I regained my senses and missed his chance of finishing with the first group. I have never forgotten that act of comradeship.

After sixteen days on Okinawa, Sergeant Little assembled us together and broke the news we all knew was coming. We were going to Vietnam. We were to be packed and loaded in forty-eight hours. We were encouraged to get our affairs in order including listing who to contact in case of...

Third Battalion was to float off the coast of Vietnam, and if trouble broke out anywhere, would go in at a moment's notice. I remember thinking that I was well trained and that nothing was ever going to hurt me. I was invincible. What a life this was turning out to be!

Chapter Five
Floating on the
USS Iwo Jima

At Buckner Bay on the southeast coast of Okinawa, the Seventh Marines boarded a new helicopter carrier, the *USS Iwo Jima*. We were headed to the waters off of the Republic of South Vietnam. Our battalion, the 3-7, was designated as a Special Landing Force (SLF) and would be available for deployment as the need presented itself.

The *Iwo Jima* was everything that the *Valley Forge* wasn't. What a ship — very Marine friendly. The living quarters were very comfortable, maybe like third class on a modern-day cruise ship. The bunks were stacked three high, instead of six, and there was plenty of room to have writing tables — actually card playing tables. The bunks were thirty-six inches wide and had civilian mattresses with fart sacks and clean sheets. The mess was well stocked and roomy. Some of the best meals I have ever eaten were aboard the *Iwo Jima*. I can still remember those huge steaks and strawberry shortcake. The rumor was the head cook was trained as a chef in Paris, France.

We never quit training no matter where we were. The few days on the high seas dictated we get everything in order. Hours were spent on the M14s, bayonets, and the gear that went into our packs. Everything such as uniforms and barracks gear were packed away in our sea bags and loaded in the hold in the bottom of the ship.

The major drills we had to do involved getting on and off the CH-34 helicopters on the flight deck. Over the loud speaker a voice would yell, "Marines, man your battle stations." We would advance in a non-panic mode to a prearranged number painted on the hanger deck in platoon formation. A sailor would then lead us up the stairs to the tower section on the flight deck. Then squad by squad we were led bent over to the helicopter. The crew chief (usually one of the machine gunners) would board us, seat us, and then have us buckle ourselves in. Then we would exit the hatch and go back down to the hanger deck and the drill would start over again the next day. Our platoon knew the hanger number red six and its location better than our own names.

On June 13, Sergeant Little assembled us and told us that as of the next day, the training ceased and the real action would begin. Staff Sergeant Little was six feet tall, 180 pounds, very muscular, intelligent, and a great leader. We were privileged to follow this Marine Corps loving man. He gave us the confidence and courage that if we followed him and would remember our training, we had a good chance of making it to fight another day. He said, "Remember, you are no good to anyone dead, especially the men who count on you. Don't die for your country. Stay alert and stay alive!" That was some speech, better than any Knute Rockne had ever given. He sure got my attention. Tomorrow there would not be paper targets; there would be live human beings that needed to be killed.

That afternoon a chaplain had church service on the hanger deck. Almost all the 1,000 Marines aboard attended. The good, the bad, the believers, the non believers, and those in between were there. Many thought, *What harm can attending church do; it would show respect and just might bring us good luck.*

The next morning, July 1, came very quickly. Our chopper lifted us off the flight deck and soared into the cloudless blue sky. I was always amazed when that ugly Korean War-era helicopter could lift ten Marines fully loaded (75-90 lbs of gear) into the bright blue yonder. It always did. The drills had paid dividends so far. We assembled in the correct place, made it to the flight deck, and into the right CH-34 without a hitch. The noise from the whirling blades was deafening. From my seat I could barely see out the hatch, and when the helicopter leaned, I could see the ground below. I could see the waves break onto the white sandy beach. Next came the greenest fields of rice, and I could make out farmers plowing with water buffaloes. There was a paved highway, and then to the south a good-sized town.

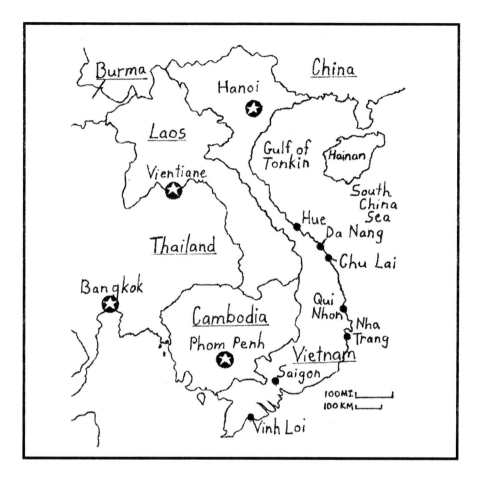

Qui Nhon, which is located on the coast about 200 miles south of Da Nang was the first place in Vietnam I visited. Most of my time in Southeast Asia was spent in and around Chu Lai. Map was provided by Ian Barnes.

After that, we started to descend into a landing zone in the hills outside the town. We hit the ground softly and started to unload. The M60 machine gunner helped us unbuckle and exit the hatch. Nobody seemed to be in a hurry. There were no explosions, or bullets in the air, no crawling on our bellies; was this war? The farmers were doing their thing, as were the town folk. Was this what was meant by the calm before the storm?

A sergeant greeted us and pointed us to India company's location. Sergeant

Little yelled at us, and we ran to join him. We had about two miles of climbing to get to our area of responsibility. It was not nearly as exhausting as Hill 921, but with all the extra gear it was not a piece of cake. We were in place as the sun started to get weak. Parks and I started to dig our foxhole and found it was nothing short of concrete. The ground was so rocky, after two hours of digging we had barely scratched the surface. We decided to place our packs in front of the eighteen-inch-deep hole and gamble on not needing much protection that first night.

There was a clearing of about half a football field in front of the rocky and barren foxhole. The terrain dropped steeply away from our position and was covered by low to medium high grass. There were islands of scrubby bushes and trees that grew to a height of no more than eight feet. At the bottom of the hill there was a narrow overgrown valley and then another steep hill, only this one was forested with larger trees. There were plenty of hiding places in front of us, and we were determined to be alert to any movement, man or animal. Our unofficial orders were to shoot first and ask questions later.

I volunteered to take the first watch at 2200 hours. I was wound tighter than piano wire, and knew I'd be awake for a while anyhow. Parks slid into his sleeping bag and got as comfortable as possible in the shallow foxhole and closed his eyes. Ten minutes later someone down the line fired off a magazine of rounds, then the next hole repeated the same, and the next, and the next. Then illumination flares were fired into the air. It seemed that the whole of Vietnam was lit up. The artillery units were firing those devices about 500 feet in front of us. The flares floated to the ground with the help of small parachutes and gave out high amounts of candle power. With the bright light, everybody opened fire. Parks came out of his bag and joined in the firing. Somebody yelled cease fire a few times and then all was quiet. Parks crawled back into his bag and tried to catch some sleep.

Not twenty minutes later, the firing started again and the lights were switched on by the artillery boys. Parks jumped out of his sleeping bag at least five times on my two-hour watch. One of the leaders, either the Gunny or Sergeant Little, would come by every hour and make sure everything was okay. Each would advise us to calm down, but if we thought we saw something, fire away. Parks had been asleep just a few minutes when I shook him and told him the good news; it was his watch now. I was asleep in no time and even all the sporadic firing the next two hours didn't bother me. Zero two hundred came too soon for me but not a second too early for Harold, who by now acted like a sleep-deprived zombie. The battalion stopped firing the illumination flares and that was fine with me. They were great if needed; however, after they fell it was hard to get my night vision back. The itchy trigger fingers had quieted, and except for an occasional visit from a leader walking the line, or a gust of wind, everything was silent.

At approximately 0330, I thought I saw something move about one hundred feet to my front left. I focused on the area where I thought I saw the movement. For fifteen minutes there was dead quiet, and then I heard a definite rattle coming from my front left. Then I saw something move. I slid as low as I could behind the small pile of dirt and rocks and pack. I wished we had put forth more effort and had dug a deeper hole. I was totally fixated on the front when this tall Viet Cong took one step to his left. He had a silly grin that revealed a gold tooth and a bushy mustache that reminded me of the Russian dictator Stalin. I kicked Parks and whispered that there was a VC, 100 feet at ten o'clock. Before Harold could get out of his sleeping bag, the enemy soldier lunged forward. I emptied twenty rounds into him, but I didn't see him fall or hear him scream out in pain. My firing startled the whole company, and it took many moments for everyone to stop firing. My partner asked, "Where is the VC?" I pointed to the spot. Not three minutes later Harold was really concentrating and saw another VC move. He opened fire, and on cue the men on our line did also. Quiet enveloped the area after everybody had his time of firing. We figured these probes were finished for the night, or at least hoped so.

About 0500 the word was passed down the line that a recon patrol would enter our lines soon and we should be careful not to shoot them. A few minutes later, daylight started to appear just slightly. I figured that in a few more minutes we could go down and see how a dead man looked. I was eighteen and already a killer. I felt no remorse over what had happened. This man was trying to kill my friends and me. Now there was one less potential American killer in the Republic of South Vietnam.

At 0530 the sun started to show itself and spread enough light for us to go down and investigate the KIA. We carefully made our way about one hundred feet and started looking for him, or maybe them. There was nothing there. We hunted for signs of blood or foot prints or marks where someone had been dragged off. Then Harold said, "Look at all these bullet holes in this tree." We had killed a tree! I had concentrated so hard on an area and some noise that was probably wind. My imagination convinced me a white-eyed, rifle-toting Viet Cong was coming toward me. We had let a bush tree ruin our first night in country. What if one of my rounds had hit one of the recon patrollers?

The next day we could see some fighting involving the South Vietnamese Army (ARVN) down below us. That was the closest we came to combat while at Qui Nhon. The US Army was getting this town with its big airport ready to receive thousands of its own troops. They needed our help. Years later I found out why we were sent so far south of our area of responsibility, which was called I Corps. According to an artillery officer by the name of Ken Sympson, in his book *Images From the Otherland*, the Army had landed and it dawned on someone that they were absent their equipment and big guns. Some hot shot clerk had failed to send the Army and their stuff together! To think, I owed some Army goof-off for that terrible, sleepless night when I killed a tree!

After a few days on guard we were flown back to the ship. The showers, clean sheets, and the chef-prepared food were much appreciated. The next few days were spent cleaning up and doing little else. We were always on call, but it never came. Seven days later the Colonel threw a beach party for us on shore. Somebody would now protect us while we goofed off. After another week of sailing up and down the coast, the ship was ordered to resupply at Subic Bay, Phillipines.

While the Navy reloaded their stores, the Marines were supposed to attend jungle warfare and survival school. It included four days in the jungle and existing off the land. When we pulled into Subic, I thought the base was right out of Hollywood. The grass was thick and manicured just like a golf course. The streets were wide and lined with huge magnificent old oak trees. The buildings had that colonial "Singapore Look" with louvered doors and windows that allowed air to circulate freely. What a beautiful place. We never got around to the school; Colonel Bodley promised to bring us back, but we did spend two days off the ship and on the base.

One of the two days was spent swimming in the bay. I lost a valuable friend that day — my class ring. When I came up out of the water and noticed it gone, I felt like I had lost a family member. I wore that ring with more pride than I had earned. I thought the ring told my peers that I was no "dummy." Now I would have to repeat the spiel about Mrs. Roark...I knew somehow, someway, I had to get a diploma. I had tried to take the GED test at Camp Geiger but missed it the week we flew to California. While at Pendleton I was scheduled to take the test but was shipped to Okinawa the week of the test. On Okinawa the education officer had me down to take it, but I missed the appointment because of our sudden departure for Vietnam. Whatever it took, I was determined to get that diploma!

We left Subic in a hurry. The Navy had a cruiser or destroyer grounded on a reef outside of Taiwan and needed the assistance of our helicopters. After a few days there, we sailed to the port of all ports, Hong Kong. It was early August and we would have seven days to live it up. Most of us had plenty of money because it had been nearly a month since our last liberty.

The ship dropped anchor about two miles out in the bay. Lance, Parks, and I caught the motor launch to the largest pier I'd ever seen. Fenwick Pier it was called, and I remember being in awe at the number of big clocks it had, one for each time zone in the world. We walked off the pier and in no time were in the middle of the most crowded place in the world.

For a kid from East Tennessee, this place of contrasts was absolutely unbelievable. The tall modern skyscrapers with bamboo scaffolding, wealthy beautiful people, squalid poverty, sincere hard working people, and the world's best cons were on the same street. I bought a Rolex watch from one of those con artists for $4. After a while it ran down and I opened the back and found its mechanism was run by a rubber band. Four dollars doesn't sound like much, but it was more than a day's pay in 1965. Most of the people were honest and hard working. I bought a sharkskin tailor made suit for $33. I paid for it in advance, and when I went back a few days later to pick it up, it was ready. We ate at some of the best restaurants in the Orient. We visited the Suzy Wong Restaurant which was named after the movie staring William Holden. My favorite eating place was Jimmy's Kitchen, an upscale swanky establishment where we enjoyed a ten-ounce filet mignon, baked potato, apple pie, and iced tea for less than $3. Hong Kong folks treated us like kings. We would go into one of their places of business and they wouldn't be able to hold back their excitement.

For all its beauty and sophistication, Hong Kong had an ugly side. When we got off the main streets, the filth and squalor were horrible. Many of the people were so poor they rummaged in garbage cans for food. Some lived on small boats no larger than half the size of a bedroom. They ate, slept, and played on those boats and some never got off them their entire lives. Women of all ages were selling themselves. One that I will never forget weighed about 70 pounds and had to be 65 years old. That was somebody's grandmother. I thought, *What an honor and privilege it is to be an American and not have to live the life most of these people do.*

One morning we met a group of British Marines who were stationed there. They offered to show us around and we accepted. One of them had a small English car about the size of a Volkswagen and it held seven, uncomfortably. They were great guides. We helped with the "petrol," as they called gas, and spent four hours touring the popular places of the British colony. They wanted to know all about us and we wanted to know about them. Those blokes had to sign up for much longer tours in their service. They spent as long as ten years away from England at a time. Their pay was considerably less than ours; however, they loved being in the Royal Marines and stationed in the exotic city of Hong Kong. We ended our time together at a back street grill that served their favorite food — fried cod and french fries or, as they called them, fish and chips.

The last day in Hong Kong was spent aboard ship. I was getting low on funds and had seen what I wanted to, so I slept in. The next morning we were headed back to Subic Bay to resupply the ship's stores. Late on the thirteenth of August, the *Iwo Jima* docked. We were given liberty the next day in Olongapo, which is located just outside the Naval base. We were warned that this city was known as the sin capital of the world. Only the main street was open to servicemen, and if we did venture off it, we faced brig time. There were stories about sailors and Marines being rolled, and some even killed for the small amount of money they carried.

We received two weeks pay and Lance, a few guys, and myself saluted the ship's flag and walked off the ship toward Olongapo. I remember thinking as we were leaving the base that I would rather stay on base, eat at the club and go bowling. I sure wished I had listened to my instincts, but the bottom line was that I wanted to be with the guys that night, and I was a follower. Outside the gate was this nasty river with kids begging us to throw a dime in the water so they could dive in and retrieve it. We passed on and left a bunch of cons, hucksters, and beggars to bother somebody else. If we had given to one, all of them would have swarmed us.

We found a clean bar and started drinking San Miguel beer. I'm not sure if it was the heat, humidity, lack of air conditioning, or that the beer was served ice cold from a freezer, but that was the only alcoholic beverage I ever enjoyed. This place had a band and they played and sang "Your Cheating' Heart" by Hank Williams over and over. After another round of drinks, a photographer took our picture for a quarter and a street vendor came in and sold us a stick of monkey meat. We had not eaten since lunch and the stick looked tasty. Each of us thought it tasted like thick bacon wrapped onto a stick. About fifteen minutes later one of the barmaids came over and told us we should be careful about buying food from these people. This particular vender, according to her, had never seen a monkey! Supposedly, he got his meat from trapping stray dogs at the dump and off the streets. Yuck!!

I am in a bar in Olongapo with PFCs Lance, Shrader, and Mclean.

After dark, Lance and I started walking around the town looking for anyone else from our company. We spotted Corporal Sanchez drinking by himself. Sanchez was a fire team leader in our platoon. He was a Filipino, small, squared away, and was making the Corps his career. Everybody liked him. We sat down next to him and both of us ordered vodka and grapefruit juice. Sanchez soon had to leave, and in order that we would not be offended, he bought us a fifth of Manila vodka.

I never learned how to drink properly. Instead of sipping, I chug-a-lugged. The taste was so terrible, the only way I could get it down was to take big swallows. I kept drinking my original glass down half way and filling it back with that rot gut vodka. I remember thinking how much I hated doing that, but the bar was full of sailors and Marines. I was determined to show everyone there that I was a man who could drink with anyone. At least five times I drank the big glass down to half and refilled it.

I remember my bladder being at the bursting point. I made it to the head just in time; it took forever for me to empty. I walked back out into the bar and spotted four sailors in a booth. I remember thinking my granddad would like to talk with those *sinners*. I made it over to them and leaned against their table. I told those young sailors that they were headed straight for hell, and if they weren't willing to change their ways they would spend eternity there. Usually Marines and sailors look for excuses to pound on each other, but all four agreed they needed to change their ways. That was the last thing I remember of August 14, 1965.

The next day, Lance told me the shore patrol came into the bar around 2200 hours and announced for all the men on the *Iwo Jima* to get back to the ship immediately. We went outside and hailed a jitney, which was a war surplus jeep converted into a taxi. The driver was told to get us to the *Iwo Jima* pronto. He must have noticed how wasted I was, because I had trouble getting in the back. I rode up front with the Fillipino. After two blocks the driver turned onto a side street. Lance was sure we were about to be rolled and left in some alley. Lance screamed that he had a 45 pistol inside his shirt and would blow the little man's head off if he didn't turn around immediately! The little fellow believed him and whipped the jeep around and deposited us in front of the ship.

By now I couldn't walk. I slid out of the seat and onto the asphalt pavement face down. Ashamedly, I was carried aboard ship. The company gunnery sergeant was there checking us in. Except for my granddad, I would rather anyone other than the Gunny see me that way. This man was six feet tall and weighed about 225 pounds. He was a Native American and reminded me of the profile on the Indian head nickel, only with a flat top. He almost never smiled and only spoke when it was necessary. That night he chose to speak to me. I was dressed down and belittled like I deserved. I was up for promotion the next month and now I was sure I would be passed over. The only good thing about the chewing out — I didn't remember a thing.

The lights came on in our quarters about 0600. I noticed the ship was moving at breakneck speed and bouncing all over the water. I felt awful and didn't remember how I got to my bunk. I was fully dressed, and I noticed my bed was soppy wet and there was green scummy watery stuff on top of the blanket. I had wet the bed like some baby and had thrown up at least a hundred times. I am thankful I slept on my side because I could have choked to death in my vomit.

I waited until every one had gone upstairs to breakfast, then I rolled out and swapped my mattress and bedding with an empty one. This took all of my energy, and I had to lie back down for a few minutes. Then I crawled up to the shower and cleaned myself. By then I was starving and somehow stumbled to the mess hall. The only thing I had eaten in the last eighteen hours was that monkey meat. I poured a cup of milk and took two bites of toast. Not two minutes later, I had to run to the head to keep from throwing up in the mess room. I was now totally exhausted, but somehow made it back to my bunk.

It was Sunday and I was allowed to lie down for the entire morning. I wanted to sleep, but the ship was moving too erratically and my head was pounding. Lance came down to my bunk and told me what had happened to us the night before. He also told me of our destination. We were heading for Vietnam to do battle with the Viet Cong. We both agreed that if he hadn't been slightly sober and bluffed the jitney driver, we might be lying in some back alley dead. Worse, we might have missed the ship and be facing court martial for missing a movement during wartime. What a dummy I was.

I thought, all this pain, sickness, and misery was just to prove my manhood. Actually, I proved the opposite; a real man wouldn't act like I had. I was a follower, too weak to do what I wanted. I hated alcohol, it hated me and yet I still drank because I wanted to be one of the guys. I determined that August 14 would be my final time to drink. I really didn't have anything to prove. I almost got killed, I could have died in my vomit, I lost what respect the Gunny ever had for me, I lost my promotion, I was sicker than at anytime in my life, and I had wet the bed like a two-year-old — just to be one of the men. If it took drinking to make me a man, I would stay a boy. That conversation I had with myself was thirty-eight years ago, and I have been alcohol free ever since.

Somehow through all of the misery I fell asleep for a couple of hours. I woke up to the most awesome aroma. It smelled like charcoal and grease burning. The chef had brought out the grills and was grilling huge steaks on the hanger deck. He knew where we were headed and wanted to send us off with a fantastic meal. I had never been so hungry and dehydrated in my life. I was sure lunch would fix all of my ills.

I wobbled up to the deck and picked out a ribeye, a potato the size of my foot, and my favorite dessert, which was strawberry shortcake with real whipped cream topping. I sat down in a quiet corner and started eating very cautiously. Two bites of steak and I got an explosive feeling in the top of my stomach that told me I had thirty seconds to get to the head. I made it just in time and lost more green stuff. Where was this stuff coming from since I hadn't eaten in twenty-four hours? I couldn't make it back to where my full tray sat. I hoped the chef wasn't offended that I wasted that great meal.

I laid back down and tried to sleep off the sickness. I was so exhausted from the last trip to puke, I just knew I would pass out and wake up rested. I was wrong as usual; I couldn't get comfortable and I hurt too much to drop off to sleep. The ship was really rocking, and my head throbbed like a piston straining to make it to the top of a steep hill. The five hours between lunch and supper lasted forever. Somehow I made it to chow and tried to keep down a piece of bread and a cup of Kool Aid. It stayed down for thirty minutes and again, I found myself vomiting my head off. That night was one of the most miserable ones of my young life. All night long my stomach screamed and my head felt like it would explode.

Morning came and I finally was able to keep something down. In retrospect, I probably experienced alcohol poisoning, or maybe I have a gene that is allergic to alcohol. What a dumb thing for me to binge drink when I knew it would hurt me. I have read of college students overdrinking and dying. How would my folks ever understand and cope if they had received a telegram that regretted to notify them that their son PFC John Kington had died due to acute alcohol poisoning? Thank you God for watching over me when I totally did not deserve Your attention.

Chapter Six
Into the Fray

Our battalion commander, Lt Colonel Bodley, had flown to Chu Lai while we were still in Subic Bay. He was there to participate in planning a major battle against the Viet Cong. Chu Lai was an air base for the Marine Air Wing located about 50 miles south of Da Nang. We were told the base was named using Chinese for Lt. General Krulak, who was the commander of all Marines in the Pacific Area. In August 1965, it was little more than a wilderness outpost with no permanent buildings, only tents and sand bag bunkers. The runway was short and paved with thousands of sections of sheet metal attached together. There were plenty of planes and helicopters stationed there and a sizable fuel and ammunition dump. A Viet Cong deserter had volunteered that a full regiment of Viet Cong was digging in around the Van Tuong village complex located some twelve miles south of Chu Lai. He said the eventual objective was to overrun the air base. The brass decided to get them before they got us.

The *Iwo Jima* anchored about ten miles off the coast of Chu Lai. Colonel Bodley laid out the game plan. Two battalions who were guarding the air base would flush the VC out into the open. Second Battalion, Fourth Marines would be helo lifted to areas west of the villages and drive toward the sea. Most of Third Battalion Third Marines would make an amphibious landing and block the sea escape route of the enemy and march inland. On the second day of the battle, Third Battalion Seventh Marines would send in four companies, two by air and two by sea. Our landing positions were calculated to put a stranglehold on the First Viet Cong Regiment, seal their escape lanes, and kill them. This would be the first large-scale battle of the war. We needed to send Hanoi a clear message. There were supposed to be at least two thousand enemy troops trapped and it would be up to our battalion to destroy them. The original idea was to use the two battalions who had been in country since May as blocking forces and use us as sweepers. We had been aboard ship for two months and were well rested. The name of this battle would be Operation Starlite.

D-Day was early morning August 18, 1965. The two battalions were landed and encountered little resistance in the beginning. One company, however, was helicopter landed on top of a VC battalion headquarters and had a field day killing the enemy. Another company of Fourth Marines caught over one hundred surprised Charlies in an open field and wiped out most of them. The two battalions were in their pincher tactic, clearing out villages and moving to cut off all avenues of escape. A village named An Cuong put up heavy resistance and paid a heavy toll. Fifty VC were counted dead there. Some Marine tanks were introduced to the battle around a small village with hills surrounding it. Charlie had counted on that movement and was waiting with mortars and 106 recoilless rifles. The convoy was stuck and being picked off by the VC artillery. Another company seemed to be trapped to the west. Lima company, from our group, was committed ahead of schedule to relieve the convoy and to assist the trapped Marines to the west. The last helicopter left the ship at a little past 1600 hours.

All day we were on standby to fly into the fray. Our packs were packed, rifles cleaned, ammo in the magazines, and grenades attached to the cartridge belts. We were ready to prove ourselves. The flight deck was unreal with the activity of helicopters landing and taking off. The pilots were bringing back reports of the fighting. They reported there were some very hot places. The Marines were really kicking butt and we were all proud, excited, and anxious to join them before they killed all the bad guys.

Then the realization of death set in. A chopper brought in some dead Marines from the battlefield. They were in olive, drab, plastic body bags with a six foot zipper in front. I was on the hanger deck as two sailors carried down the first Marine. They were laughing and joking. One said something like, "I'll bet these big bad Marines aren't so anxious to leave the ship now."

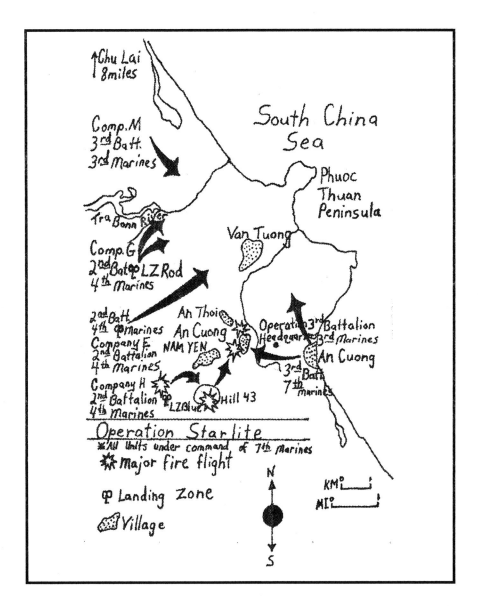

The operation map of Operation Starlite which was the first major battle of the Vietnam War. My company, India 3-7, landed on the west side of the coastal village of An Cuong. Map is courtesy of Ian Barnes.

We were in formation and couldn't break, but those of us who heard them determined not to rest until those swabbies learned a lesson in respect. I never saw either one of them again. I was both angry and apprehensive at the same time, but understood dying was for others to experience. I was young and invincible and knew nothing would happen to me.

Early on the morning of August 19,1965, India company was flown off the flight deck and into the first large battle of the Vietnam War. We flew over the most beautiful aqua blue water and white beaches I had ever seen. The water and beaches reminded me of the Gulf of Mexico and Pensacola, Florida. The inland area was flat for the most part but included some high ground, randomly placed in the middle of lush green rice paddies. The natives in their bamboo and straw thatched huts lived on the higher land.

The whirling blades were extremely loud. The noise seemed to climb under our helmets and amplify. Communication was impossible except for hand gestures. The morning was already hot and steamy, but the wind rushing through the open hatch felt good. The M60 gunners were focused and alert. The machine guns were bolted to the floor with plenty of ammo in metal boxes nearby. With the concentration of M60 fire, death was almost certain for the VC, or at least they wished they were dead. This was not going to be like Qui Nhon where we sat in foxholes most of the time.

The CH-34s landed in the middle of a wet rice field. The gunners started helping (actually throwing) us out the hatch. The flyboys were taking incoming fire and wanted to get airborne as soon as possible. We were knee deep in water and loaded down with flak jackets, helmets, full packs, rifles, and ammo belts. I hit the ground and could barely move my legs in the oozy muck. Our leaders were yelling, "hurry, run, move, get out of there!" but we could only move as fast as water, muck, and our strength would allow. I sure was glad no one was shooting at us. We finally got out of the quicksand-like goo and set up a perimeter around the landing zone to wait for the rest of India to arrive.

As soon as the rest of the guys landed, the Captain yelled for us to saddle up and move out. Our first objective was to hookup with Lima company about four miles away. An hour had passed and no one had fired at us. We heard plenty of battle noise in the distance, such as artillery explosions and small arms fire. Sergeant Little continually warned us to be quiet and watch where we were stepping. Another hour and we were out of the rice paddies and on a sandy plain with a few small hills. We were now taking incoming rounds with regularity. Each time the column was fired upon, we stopped and a unit would be sent out to locate the enemy. On one occasion a platoon from India was dispatched out to find Charlie. They did, and killed quite a few. Most of the time, however, the pint-sized enemy ran instead of standing and fighting. Being fired upon happened so many times, we started not ducking at the incoming rounds. That was dangerous!

The choppers were landing at prearranged sites and resupplying us, mostly with water and ammo. We were supposed to drink eight canteens per day. The humidity was extremely high and having to hump all of our gear, ammo, rifle, and packs caused us to perspire rivers of sweat. The item that caused the most grief was the flak jacket. It was not only heavy and bulky, but the material was of dark green nylon that seemed to soak up the heat. Without the constant intake of water, dehydration set in quickly. Most of the medical evacs that first day were from heat-related sickness. The *Iwo Jima* was air conditioned and most of us were not used to the combination of heat and humidity.

Around 1300 hours we took a lunch break. My fire team set up in a clump of trees and removed our packs. Three hours of high adrenalin and the hot sun, which had caused the temperature to rise close to 100 degrees, had me in a starving mode. I prepared my c-rations and noticed ten feet away lay seven dead young VC fighters. A couple of them looked to be no more than fifteen years old. They were all dressed in black pajamas, had hair on the top of their heads and shaved slick on the sides above their ears. Most Vietnamese men wore their hair like the cartoon character Bart Simpson. There were flies galore amid the stench of the rotting and bloated torsos. Those dead, skinny boys were missing eyes, arms, noses, and other vital parts. The whole area was sickening. I had no problem, however, eating my meal and smoking two of the four free cigarettes issued in the c-ration box. I asked myself, *Am I just tired and hungry, or have I become stone cold to this carnage with only a few hours of exposure to battle?*

That day we marched at least four miles in order to connect with Lima. Stopping at each rifle shot was getting to everyone. At each village we had to enter all the huts and hunt for signs of Charlie. Most had only women, old people, and very young kids. The young men were either VC or conscripted to help them as load bearers and stretcher carriers. The only sign of the enemy we found was underground in what the villagers called the bomb shelters. Bill Van Zanten, India's executive officer, in his book *Don't Bunch Up*, remembered us detonating an explosive in one shelter. Billows of smoke rose four hundred feet away from at least eight different holes! A tunnel that large, and yet, there were no signs of the piles of dirt that had been removed. These people were masters of camouflage. After dark and way behind schedule, we met up with Lima. On a hillside we dug in and waited for Victor Charlie to attack. He never showed up.

The first day of the battle, over six hundred Viet Cong lost their lives. The next five days saw only fifty of them killed, and India was credited with a third of those KIAs. It was obvious to everyone that Charlie had learned a valuable lesson. Don't stand and fight these Devil Dogs, as the Germans once called us. The First Viet Cong Regiment with its four battalions had escaped our trap. They did that by disbanding their units and going into hiding. The Fourth and Third Marines were airlifted back to Chu Lai on the third day and left the clean-up to us.

The next four days were no fun at all. The objective was to mop up the stragglers from the VC Regiment, but they were long gone. They even stopped shooting at us and running away. We were forever moving out. Each time "intelligence" thought they had located the enemy, we were dispatched. One day a fighter pilot reported seeing secondary explosions close to his bombing run. They were sure this was the area where the enemy ammo dumps were located. We forced marched four miles, fully loaded in temperatures that hovered in the high 90s. It was a false alarm! On the trip, some of the guys took off their long-sleeved utility shirts and stowed them in their packs. Colonel Bodley ordered everyone to put the shirts back on. He barked, "You should look like Marines no matter the location or circumstance!"

Operation Starlite was a learning experience for not only the Viet Cong, but us as well. Usually the heat was more of an enemy than Charlie. Water was to be treated with iodine tablets and then sipped and not chug-a-lugged. We were warned not to drink out of the rice paddies or streams. We were constantly in some type of water and had to be careful with our feet and legs. If we didn't check often, a leech could suck too much blood and leave us weak and infected. Clean socks were a must to fight blisters. One of the most important things learned was in order to be a valuable fighter we had to take care of not only our fighting tools, but the ones carrying those tools.

Starlite was declared a great victory for the Americans and especially the Marines. President Johnson awarded us the Presidential Unit Citation, and the Secretary of the Navy presented our battalion with the Navy Unit Commendation. The military newspaper, *Stars and Stripes*, reported the battle in exciting detail for weeks. Rarely did anyone mention anything about those dead Marines who were flown aboard the *Iwo Jima*. America lost forty-six great young men that week. Seven hundred enemy dead were not nearly enough to offset our loss. We wouldn't catch the guerillas in regiment-size battle again until March 21, 1966.

The battalion flew back to the ship, picked up the rest of our gear, and after a few days was transported to the air base at Chu Lai. I would spend the next seven months in and around there. The airstrip area was devoid of any vegetation, just dirty brown dusty sand. Sand bag bunkers partially built were placed every fifty feet surrounding the entire airstrip. Our fire team settled into a bunker that was midpoint along the strip. Those bunkers were eight by eight feet and five feet high with two feet below ground. If we dug deeper than two feet the hole filled up with water. Being a little below ground provided some semblance of cool and shade. They were roofed with tin strips that were covered with more sand bags. We probably filled more sand bags at Chu Lai than are on the Mississippi River levy.

The battalion erected a mess tent about fifteen hundred yards from our bunker. Three good, hot meals each day sure did beat c-rations. We found a good use for the miserable sand. It was great to clean our slick tin mess gear. A huge problem was keeping the rifles clean. The dusty sand played havoc with the ammo also. There were natives outside the gate always selling something. One day this kid showed up with some rifle bags that had been made from scrap plastic. They had watched us constantly cleaning our stuff and decided they could help and at the same time make a buck. For one dollar, we had a cover for our rifles that lasted for weeks before the plastic would harden and start to crack. Those people could take our scrap and make all kinds of things with it. Just out of old empty beer cans, they made lamps, boxes, trunks, roofs, shelters, and more. The Vietnamese would take our discarded tires and make shoes, covers, and door hinges. Anything we threw away, even food, they found a use for it.

During the next couple of weeks we finished sand bagging the bunkers. We stood guard each night, and when not on a work detail, played cards most of the day. My system of gin rummy was becoming unbeatable. The more practice I had the better I became. At a penny a point I was pocketing a few dollars almost every day. With combat pay I was drawing less than $140 a month and with the winnings I felt rich. The only problem was, there was no place to spend all the money. There were plenty of poker games floating, and when I learned how to play and bluff, I did well there also. I found it was easy to bluff if I had plenty of money in my pocket. I learned the game of pinochle on the air strip and would rather play it than pad my earnings.

No matter what we did, the dust, heat, and jet noise seemed unbearable. Some of the guys sent their laundry out with some of the enterprising Vietnamese women at the front gate. I was always afraid if we pulled out, I would be unable to find the mama san with my clothes. I washed mine the old-fashioned way, in my helmet. The Seabees set up some portable showers toward the end of our second week there and they sure made a difference.

One night in early September, Sgt Little gathered the platoon around him and told us we were going back into the Van Tuong complex. We would finish off the First Viet Cong Regiment this time. They named the operation Piranha, after the man-eating fish. Our battalion would land two companies by sea and two by air. We would then pinch the VC into the open and finish what we wanted to do on Operation Starlite. India was helo lifted off in the early afternoon. This was the sixth time I had flown over Vietnam and still I was awestruck at its beauty.

We had been flying for about fifteen minutes at 2,000 feet when I felt a terrific jolt. The chopper was in an area where ground fire was common. The loud noise of the engine and the whirling blades stopped. I could see into the bottom of the cockpit and thought I saw panic. The pilots were frantically stomping on the pedals trying to restart the engine! We were dropping like a lead balloon! We were going to crash and I knew death was certain. My life history flashed in front of me. All of those stupid, dumb things I had done were playing out in front of me in slow motion. I started to pray. I told God that if he saved us I would never smoke another cigarette again. My parents and grandparents hated that I smoked and I felt guilty each time I lit up. About five hundred feet above the ground, the pilot got the engine started and the blades began the whirling noise, but we were still falling. Instead of landing, the pilots were wrestling with the chopper by flying huge circles at three hundred feet, then two hundred and finally one hundred feet. Close to the ground, the pilots got everything under control. We landed hard, but we did land. Whew!

For years, I thought the sudden drop was maybe a pilot's tactic to get us down quickly and avoid all the ground fire. Steve LeMarr, an Army pilot in Vietnam, told me that move was much too risky. He remembered some of the Marine pilots in helicopter school using a similar technique in order to drop faster, but never with a heavy load such as ten fully loaded Marines. Also the move would not work on an old bulky cargo helicopter such as the CH-34. I have been remiss all these years for not properly giving my Maker all the credit due Him.

We jumped out of the hatch onto dry land and set up a perimeter around the landing zone. The two guys on each side of me lit up cigarettes. After about two minutes, the aroma of those cigarettes was the sweetest smell I had ever smelled. I wanted a smoke so badly, but I had just promised God I would quit smoking. He had just saved our lives. I knew how a heroin addict felt when he was craving a fix. I couldn't believe how much I wanted a Winston. I closed my eyes and thought, *Get a hold of yourself. Think, does God want you in a battle zone and nervous? Which one would be worse? Nervous and dying and maybe causing a friend to get killed, or calm and smoking?* I rationalized it would be okay for me to smoke, so I lit up. I had just made a promise to God and couldn't keep it for five minutes. I carried that guilt for my whole tour of duty in Vietnam.

Operation Piranha was not nearly the success that Starlite was. We did capture and kill a few of the guerillas. We found some weapons caches, and destroyed plenty of tunnels, but were generally disappointed with the results. Almost every village in the Van Tuong complex had underground hiding places. There were at least 1,000 VC still in the area, but they didn't want any part of us. We figured they had just melted into the local population or were hiding in the tunnels. When they would fire at us, it was from usually 300 or 400 feet away. They never fired over three or four shots before running away. Instead of fighting, they ran, and in doing so, lived another day. They were frustrating us to no end.

I remember three things about Piranha in addition to the near helicopter crash. The first memory was how jaded we all had become. Being fired on became so commonplace we rarely even considered the source. Actually most of the time we didn't flinch. Our thinking was, if you heard the gunfire, that was good because the shot that kills is never heard.

The second memory happened at 0300 hours one morning. We were to act as a blocking force for another company that would sweep Charlie toward us. We had to pass through a village that was known to support the VC. As our group approached the outskirts, word was passed down the column to shoot anything that moved, be it man, woman, or child. Parks was behind me and whispered, "I ain't going to shoot no baby, no matter what happens."

The village must have known we were coming because everyone stayed inside. They were huddled around a candle and made sure we could see they were no danger to us. The women were crying and holding their children tightly. They were terrified of us that night. Would I have killed a youngster if he or she came outside and was close to me? I don't know. What a responsibility to put on an eighteen-year-old!

The last memory took place on the final day of the operation. All of us were scummy, filthy, dirty. We stank so bad, ambushes were out of the question. All were sure that Charlie could smell us within 200 yards. The battalion was located about 2000 yards west of the South China Sea. Colonel Bodley decided for hygiene sake, we would march to a well-protected area and clean up. We dropped our clothes, grabbed a bar of soap from our packs and ran into the water. In mid September, the water temperature was around 90 degrees. In about three feet of water I just sat down and let my achy joints enjoy the moment. Lathering in the salty water opened every pore in my body. That time in the water was one of the most relaxing moments I had ever experienced. I thought, *After we win this war and I become wealthy, I'm coming back to this exact beach and build a luxury resort.*

I had been in the Marine Corps for a little over a year. Except for a few minor incidents such as encounters with Corporal Terry, almost drowning, losing my class ring, having alcohol poisoning, and nearly dying in a helicopter crash, I was enjoying myself. I was camping out every night, had free food and clothes, and had visited some really exotic places. The thing that far outweighed everything else was all the friendships I was making. I was eighteen and what a wonderful life I had in front of me!

Chapter Seven
Echo 2-4

The remainder of September was spent building bunkers, patrolling, setting up ambushes, standing watch, and taking care of our gear. We were forever establishing new defensive lines, building sand bag bunkers, and then in a few days, moving on to a new area and starting all over again. We kept moving farther out from the air strip. Each move necessitated securing the area. This was accomplished with constant patrols thru the countryside and villages. Each village had to be searched and searched again for any signs of the enemy.

I was always amazed at the living conditions in the Vietnamese villages. In their huts many had an area devoted to Buddha. This was usually at the inside entrance with thirty-inch straws burning as incense. Most huts were one or two dirt floor rooms with no beds, only straw floor mats. Most of the time these small straw structures housed grandparents, a child and spouse, and grandchildren. They did their cooking outside and there was always a basket of rice next to the back exit. A house's wealth was measured by the size of the rice bin. Those bins were a favorite place to hide weapons. Sadly, we were forced to empty many of the bins, and the houses that contained VC assets or occupants were torched. That sounds cruel, but some of those people were trying to kill us.

Some of the larger villages had one or two concrete structures built by the

French before 1954. They were used as schools, town meeting halls, and churches. The straw houses were surprisingly solid. It was astonishing when it rained — the insides of those places would be powder dry. Most of the people were friendly and seemed to enjoy our visits, especially when we brought them food and medical attention. Almost all of the kids under the age of five were naked and barefooted. The mothers carried the diaperless babies in a sling on their backs. A funny thing was none of us remember seeing an infant wet on his mom while being carried. We wondered if the Vietnamese mothers had a special way to potty train their little ones.

The women chewed a natural narcotic substance called betel nut. The nuts were orange and came from a betel palm tree. They would chew the nut into a pulp and hold it in the front of their mouths similar to the way one would dip smokeless tobacco. By the time they reached thirty-five, their teeth were rotten to the gum line. Most of the men didn't chew until they got a lot of age on them. Some of our guys tried chewing the nut (it was found everywhere), but said the taste wasn't worth the slight high or buzz they experienced.

One morning my squad was sent out to patrol an unfamiliar area. The squad was split into two groups in order to check out more ground. We were going to meet again at 1300 hours at a prearranged point. The Marines were receiving some interpreters from the South Vietnamese Army (ARVN) to help us communicate with the locals. On this particular day we had an interpreter who looked like a fourteen-year-old kid fresh out of junior high school.

My half squad had been out for about two hours and came across a village that was not on our map. The community well looked brand new. We began cautiously searching each hut for enemy signs. The interpreter was asked to find the chief and determine from where all the people came. A six-foot, well-fed, high-cheekboned, forty-five-year-old Vietnamese claimed to speak for everyone. This dude did not look like the small typical Vietnamese man. He said his group had broken away from another village about three miles away almost two years earlier. They picked this place because of the plentiful supply of water for rice growing. He volunteered that all of the villagers hated the VC. Our whole group noticed the interpreter acted extremely afraid and subservient to the chief. The Vietnamese leader spoke very loudly and was animated with the fourteen-year-old. The little guy kept moving his head up and down in nervous agreement. When we questioned him about his behavior, he indicated nothing was wrong. He told us the best route to the east meeting point was around to the left of the village and past an outcropping of rock. We were going that way anyway.

As we proceeded to the rocks, the contour of the land gradually rose about twenty-five feet. The interpreter started walking to the rear of the group. One of us yelled, "Get on up here or you will be left behind." He yelled that he would catch up with us. The kid claimed he had to relieve himself.

We were about 250 feet outside the village when we were startled by incoming rounds! The shots were coming from no more than thirty feet away! It was a miracle that none of us were hit. We dove to the ground behind some rocks and started returning fire. Next, a couple of guys crawled to the shooters' left flank and opened fire. One VC was killed and another was wounded, but somehow escaped. He left his weapon and a lot of blood on the ground. We searched everywhere, but that Charlie had disappeared into thin air.

We rolled over the dead man, and to our astonishment, it was the six-foot-tall village chief! That cowardly little interpreter had led us into a trap. We found him where he was supposed to be taking a leak. He was on the ground shivering as if he had a high fever. One of us picked up his eighty-pound body by the back of his neck and dragged him up to the squad leader. We were really angry, yet at the same time had pity for the kid. We kept calling him a VC and he started crying and repeating over and over that he hated the Viet Cong. Now where had I heard that before?

He may not have been on the other side, but he almost got some of us killed by being a coward. The squad leader told us, "Leave him alone; the people at headquarters will take care of the little gook." A chopper was called in to take him back to the rear to be interrogated. When the helicopter landed, two guys literally threw him inside and told the gunner this kid probably was Viet Cong. I never heard from the boy again. If the questioners turned him over to the ARVN, he would be sent to a prison camp, or worse, maybe shot for being a traitor. Looking back, we should have felt sorry for the youngster, but in 1965 the feeling was more like rage.

Why had these people ambushed us? The two weapons we captured were old rusty twenty-two calibers. I would have been afraid to fire them because of the gunk on the inside and outside of the rifles. There were six of us, each with an M14, 120 rounds of ammo, and four or five hand grenades. Our M14s would fire one round at a time or could be switched to automatic and fire just like a machine gun. They risked almost certain death and for what? The enemy kept learning from their mistakes. That was one of the few times their firing range against us was less than 400 feet away.

In late September or early October, India was brought back to the air base and set up operations in large tents next to the South China Sea. There was always Marine stuff to do, but plenty of time to swim, participate in physical games, and play cards. The best things about being on the beach were the absence of mosquitoes and little or no standing watch. In the past, we were nightly standing foxhole watch or staying awake on ambushes. Now we were sleeping all night on a canvas cot. That luxury seemed too good to be true.

A week later a few of us were told to pack our bags and report about a half mile away to Second Battalion, Fourth Marines. I had been with India for almost five months and hated to leave my friends, but understood that I was one of its newer members and should be the first to be transferred if somebody had to be. Later I learned that almost all of India company was integrated into existing units that had been in Southeast Asia since the first of May.

A bunch of us walked to a sandy hilltop where our new battalion was deployed. Tom (Top Cat) Gardner and I reported and were assigned to Echo Company, which placed us in First Lieutenant Gary Brown's platoon. I ended up in Corporal Allen's fire team along with Chester Gafkowski and Private James Imel from Anderson, Indiana. Allen was a black man from Chicago who was well liked and very squared away. Years later I heard Ed Brummett remark that Allen was the best point he ever knew.

Gafkowski was a month younger than I and was from Brooklyn. It took four days for us to understand each other's accent. "Ski" was likeable, always laughing and clowning around. He worked hard, never complained, and I was proud to serve with him. It was also neat to find someone that I could call "kid." Ski was so gung-ho, he and Gardner signed up for six extra months in the war zone.

James Perry Imel was the opposite of Ski. He was serious, shy, almost never spoke, and looked even younger than Ski. Some of the guys rode him because he was always reading his Bible. That sounds bad, but sometimes when things needed to be done, such as cleaning his rifle or helping around the compound, Imel was reading. I determined this guy needed a friend and I hope I was one. I taught him to smoke. One night the temperature dropped very fast. It must have been 70 degrees and we were all freezing because we were used to it being much warmer. James smoked one of my cigars under his poncho to keep warm. I think it was his first smoke and maybe his last one.

Attending nine different schools nine straight years taught me how to make new friends quickly. Echo seemed just like India in no time. Marines are the same everywhere; we all needed a friend, even more so in Nam. At boot camp, the Corps purposely pushed us together. It was us against the world, us against the brass, us against the DIs. We were taught to take care of each other and prop up those who needed it. It was no different in Vietnam. Within two days I knew hometowns, girlfriends, histories, and goals of at least twenty guys. Everyone was just as interested in me, in my old outfit, where I was from, and if everybody from Tennessee talked the way I did.

Just like in India, we were given the choice of free beer or Cokes, two or three days each week. This was supposed to keep up our morale. I know for sure that it was so important that Seventh Marines had one officer whose main duty was accounting for the beer supply. Can you imagine a child asking his father, "Dad, what did you do in the war?"

"Son, I guarded the beer," the proud parent would reply.

No matter where we were, the Marines would find a way to get us some liquid refreshments. So many days when the temperature soared into the 90s, I craved something cold. Usually they would fly out the beer in ice chests and the Cokes in cardboard boxes. Do I take an ice cold beer or a warm Coke? I never forgot that horrible "day after" on the Iwo Jima and was never tempted to drink again. My Tennessee naiveté did make me lose my Coke ration one day. A new choice was added, cold ale. I had never heard of ale and it was cold. One sip and I gave my English beer away.

Since 1999, I have belonged to a group of retired Marines that get together a few times each month. When I first joined, everybody wanted to buy me a drink. I kept politely refusing, not wanting to tell anyone about Olongapo and how stupid I was. After about twenty refusals, a wonderful old Korean War veteran by the name of Bill Sullivan whispered, "You're on the wagon, aren't you?" I nodded yes. Bill got the word out, "Do not offer Randy a drink anymore because he is a recovering alcoholic." Nobody ever offers anymore.

Echo was doing the same things India had been doing. We were standing watch, building bunkers, patrolling, ambushing, and on and on. One thing Echo did that I had not done with India was visit Chu Lai City. A bunch of thatched huts had sprung up outside the air base. The South Vietnamese had a thriving business selling things to the Marines who passed through. The stores straddled the only paved highway (Highway One) I ever remember seeing. One day a truck load of us were passing through the town on the way to a work detail. We had crossed a rickety, old, rusty river bridge that was built by the French in the 1920s. There were old, concrete, round gun placements on each side of the road and on both ends of the bridge. They were manned by many of the old guys from India. The truck was in line and could not move, and it gave me time to visit with some old friends.

The driver finally made it into the city and pulled over and told us we had thirty minutes to get back to the truck. A few of us headed to this shop that advertised cold Coca Colas. The Coke was cool, not cold, but good enough. Actually the Vietnamese would collect and wash (I hoped) Coke bottles and fill them with their own version of the "real thing." What the heck, it was brown, fizzed, and was cool. In war one has to make sacrifices. The shopkeeper was an older Vietnamese, tall, very clean, with a long neatly trimmed gray beard. The store had a wooden floor (which was unusual) and two medium-sized rooms. Fifty feet outside the back door was a huge rice paddy complex that was watered by the river we had just crossed. The old man carried many American things such as cigarettes, sodas, cameras, film, and Zippo lighters. Mainly though, the store was full of Vietnamese staples like packaged food, fire crackers, pots, pans, candles and incense straws for Buddha.

I was browsing around and noticed in the back room the most beautiful creature I had ever seen in all of my eighteen years. She was sixteen or seventeen and was wearing a form-fitting, traditional, long silk dress, split up to her mid thigh. It was light green and buttoned high under her chin. Her skin was white, clear and smooth like satin. Her eyes were more round than slanted, making me think she was part French. Wow, I thought I might be in love. I approached her and inquired if she spoke English. She knew how to count in English but not how to speak it. One of the guys came over and told me she was the shopkeeper's daughter and he was very protective of her. I turned to her and said "parlez vous francais?" She came alive and rattled off about sixty words in French. I didn't have a clue what she was saying, but kept repeating "oui, oui" as if I did. I reached out to grab her hand, and her father came in and frightened her.

An Echo company guy came in the store and told us the truck was leaving in 10 minutes and not to be late. I turned my attention back to Miss Wonderful. The feeling I had for her was like a thirsty man who needed a drink of water. I just had to touch her arm or face in order to make sure she was real. I brought the back of my hand up to my lips and motioned if I could kiss the back of hers. I was trying to get across to her I was really a French gentleman disguised in a Marine uniform. She giggled out loud. She handed me the back of her hand and bowed her head. When I started kissing the back of her hand, she started really giggling. I then kissed her fingers and she laughed out loud. I thought I was really turning that innocent little thing on. I gave her one last exaggerated kiss on the back of her *left* hand and said goodbye and promised that I would be back.

As I was running back to the truck I thought Miss Wonderful was the kind of girl one takes home to meet the parents. I believed with a little courting this girl might be the right one for me. One of the guys told everyone in the truck that "Randy got a little hand sugar in the store." Everybody hee hawed. I wanted to know what was up. One fellow asked, "Have you ever seen a roll of toilet paper in any of the huts we've searched?" He said the Vietnamese crap in the rice paddies to make the rice grow bigger, faster, and richer. I knew what was coming next; he said they dip their *left* hand in the water to clean themselves. Yuck! No wonder she laughed so hard. I really thought she was getting excited.

It was starting to rain some and cool the stifling heat a little. Nights were comfortable compared to those in the summer when the heat and humidity caused us to stay wet all the time. With the rain, our ponchos kept us semi dry. The poncho was a eight foot square bolt of thick plastic with a hole in the middle for the head. A cover was sown in to keep the head dry. The ponchos had some problems. They were bulky and made a lot of noise. They all leaked just enough to keep us moist but not soppy wet inside. Being hot and steamy wet was almost as miserable as being cold and wet. It was hard to be agile while wearing a poncho. It was so bulky and cumbersome, being clumsy was commonplace.

One afternoon while on a regular patrol, two Vietnamese local militiamen accompanied us. They were up front between the point and myself. We were constantly on the lookout for booby traps. The rain and the slick paths made them harder to find. All of a sudden one of the militiamen grabbed the point man and yelled for everyone to stop. In broken English one said there was a VC mine in the middle of the trail. They crawled to a part of the path that was well worn and pointed to a rough spot. I looked really close and didn't see anything different from hundreds of other paths we had walked on. They took out their knives and probed around the rough place. Then gently they stuck their knives about an inch deep in the ground and flipped up a mud-covered c-ration cardboard box that hid an anti-personnel mine. It was so well camouflaged, if the point man had missed it, odds were I would not. Those things blew off feet, legs, and worse. I remembered in Okinawa when the referee tagged our fire team KIA and thinking how easy it was to not make it. In Vietnam, it was no different except here the consequences were for real. The odds of survival plummeted if we were not focused every single moment.

In October the monsoon rains came. Staying dry was impossible. The perimeter around the air base was well defined and not being expanded as much as in the past. There were the front lines which extended out from the air strip about six or seven miles. Then there were compounds behind the front and then the inner defense around the runway and hangers. Companies were constantly moving from the front to the compounds and then to the air base, and then back to the front. This movement familiarized us with the whole area.

Echo was located behind the outer front during the heavy monsoon rains. The company was stretched out over a wide area. There was a mess tent and showers set up in the center of the camp. My bunker was a mile away from the center of the company. We had two-man, leaky pup tents set up, and inside had air mattresses on which to lay our sleeping bags. At least it was better than sleeping on the ground, except when the mattress sprung a leak and we would wake up soppy wet. That occurred frequently due to the age of our "rubber ladies." Heck, it seemed everything we had was used in Korea. Many of the platoons had a central forty-by-forty-foot tent erected where we could write letters, play cards, socialize, or just hang out and stay dry. From the twenty-seventh of October to the tenth of November the rain poured twenty-fours hours each day. Our responsibility didn't end just because of the heavy rains, either. We were out patrolling, setting up ambushes, and standing watch in the rain. The visibility was almost zero. *I thought, if I am this miserable, the VC are also. Why not call a ceasefire until the rain stopped and, at least, both sides could stay dry?*

War anytime is horrible; however, in the wet and mud, the misery index approached the top of the scale. Keeping rifles and ammo in working order was of the utmost importance. The plastic rifle bags seemed to accelerate the growth of rust. I asked Dad to send some gun blue over and hopefully I could stop the rusting. I spent hours sanding out all the scratches and dents where rust grew. Then I painted the steel of the rifle and ammo magazines with the bluing stain. In the end it was all a waste of time. The gun blue seemed to cause more rust to occur in the steamy wet climate.

Keeping our feet dry and clean was as important as anything we could do. We were issued an extra pair of boots and were constantly changing them and our socks. The times we couldn't change, our feet would become solid white and skin would fall off in big pieces, then we had to worry about blisters. Someone said an army moves on its stomach. We found out good, clean, dry feet were just as important

On November 9 it had rained fourteen straight days and nights. Vietnam is very sandy and can soak up a lot of water, but now many areas were starting to flood. One day we passed by my old battalion headquarters and saw panic. The water rose about three feet overnight and flooded everything. By now, staying dry was past history. People say one can get used to about anything, and I agree. I still don't understand how I slept in that wet mud.

On November 10, 1965, the Marine Corps' birthday, we woke up to a clear sky. It was almost like a religious experience with God indicating His approval of the Corps by banishing the rain on our birthday. We spent all morning drying out clothes and gear. Lunchtime was awesome! Helicopters flew in insulated boxes of huge hot steaks with all the trimmings and a big birthday cake. Did we ever enjoy that dry party! It never rained like that again. I was driving in a storm recently and the rain came down so hard my wipers wouldn't work. I had to pull off to the side of the road because the visibility was zero. That was how we had spent fourteen days and nights in the fall of 1965.

We were fortunate to have Gary Brown as our leader. He was originally from South Carolina. Lt. Brown was bright, well organized, and a great communicator. I really liked that man. He was thin, wiry, athletic, and was well respected by the troops. He wore a short Marine hair cut, and was always squared away. His boots were always dark and his utilities usually had a crease in them even in the combat zone. After all, if our leader was sloppy then we could be also. This made him stand out as a target, but he knew the platoon would function better if we cared about our appearance. His management style was to lead by example. Some of the officers screamed and yelled to make a point, but not Mr. Brown. He used classic textbook management in treating us like he wanted to be treated. This created an atmosphere where we would do anything for that man. The last thing any of us wanted was to disappoint the platoon commander.

Sometime in the middle of November, Mr. Brown sent for me. I entered his tent after announcing myself. I was sure I hadn't done anything wrong, but maybe I had. The Lieutenant asked me about my family, the Smoky Mountains, how I was getting along in a new platoon, and did I have any problems he could help me with? Then he said, "Lance Corporal, if you ever need to talk, feel free to come by."

"Yes sir," I answered. I had just been promoted to E-3. One more grade and I would be a non-commissioned officer and could wear the honored red stripes down the sides of my dress blue trousers. I thought, *What an outstanding life the Marine Corps is giving me!*

A week later, I was summoned to Lt. Brown's tent again. The Lieutenant said he had lost his radio operator. The position was important and carried a lot of responsibility. Mr. Brown said he needed someone reliable and thought I would be a good fit. The radioman stood the same amount of watches, went on the same patrols and ambushes, only he carried fifteen more pounds on his back. I told him I didn't know anything about the radio, but if he thought I could do the job, I'd like to try it. He sent me over to Lt Williamson's operator, Fred Price, for a crash course in radio nomenclature. What a hoot that was. Fred was from Boston and both of us had to have an interpreter to understand each other. Fred's alphabet had only 25 letters — no R. The first things I learned were the call signs. The company's was Sudden Death Echo. The Captain's was Echo 6 Actual, Lt. Brown's was Echo 3 Actual, and mine was plain ole Echo 3.

I've wondered why me and the radio? Was it my Tennessee drawl? In WWII the Marines used Navaho Indians to transmit in their native language and foil the Japanese from deciphering their messages. My accent was so outrageous the other operators kept requesting that I repeat my transmissions. They couldn't believe someone born in the United States of America could talk like I did. Many times when we were in camp, other operators would bring their friends over and ask if I would speak for them. I'll bet I drove the Viet Cong that monitored our frequency crazy with "ya'll, yonder, fixin to, holler, fetch," and more.

Right before lunch on December 5, Echo was ordered to fly out south to the province of Quang Ngai, where a helicopter had gone down inside an old French fort. We didn't return to the Air Base until about 1000 hours the next day. The company accomplished its mission of protecting the crippled bird and as an unexpected bonus, destroyed a Viet Cong battalion. We only counted 17 enemy bodies, but knew from all the bloody trails that many more had died. An ARVN sweep of the area the following week uncovered 146 fresh graves according to our XO. Sadly, some of our friends were either killed or injured. Twenty-six Marines were awarded the Purple Heart and Captain Ledin was awarded the Silver Star for his leadership and bravery. I never found out how many he actually received, but the Captain had so many shrapnel wounds, he deserved at least thirty Purple Hearts (this battle is described in Chapter One).

I am so proud to have served with the men of Echo Company. I never saw one Marine use drugs or treat another person disrespectfully. We had men from both wealthy families and poor ones. There were African-Americans, Caucasians, Hispanics, and American Indians, some who were educated and some not. We were from all parts of America. Though we were all different (and I know it is a cliché), we were a group of One. The only color anyone knew was Marine Corps green. I don't ever remember us using the word love, but we did love each other and proved it every day. If any one of us were lying injured, out in the open, surrounded by mines and enemy soldiers, and the odds were ninety-nine out of a hundred against success, everyone I knew in Echo would volunteer to attempt the rescue. It was my great honor and privilege to have served in Echo Company, Second Battalion, Fourth Marines!

This photo of Third Platoon was taken around Christmas, 1965. I am missing probably because of being in Okinawa for R & R, or I may have been the one taking the photo. Sadly, quite a few of these men's names can be found on the Vietnam Veterans' War Memorial in Washington, D.C.

Chapter Eight
In The Right Place

The next duty station for Echo was an artillery outpost northwest of Chu Lai called Hill 69. Out in the middle of a flat plain surrounded by endless rice paddies rose a hill that was 69 meters high, hence the name Hill 69. It seemed as steep as the hills back at Camp Pendleton and was solid red clay. From this outpost the artillery boys could control an area five miles in any direction. The ARVN had shaved the top off the hill and dug foxholes around the top at about the sixty-five meter mark. Furthermore, they mined the bottom 75% of the hill and did not map where they laid all the explosive devices. I always thought that was a waste because the sides of the hill were covered with thick scrubby bushes. There was no way to be quiet when pushing through that undergrowth! It was also so steep a man would have to have ropes and ladders to hang onto in order to climb it. There was only one path to the top, and at about the fifty-five meter point there was a small landing. Helicopters could land there but usually chose the safer place at the bottom.

At the base of the hill was a small village that seemed to be friendly. We got to know the kids because of all the time spent at the bottom receiving the helicopters. Everything — c-rations, ammo, water, and artillery shells — had to be carried up. After a rain, the path was so slick we spent more time crawling than walking.

Each succeeding company worked on improving the bunker system. Helicopters had flown in corrugated sheets of tin to be used as roofs that would keep the bunkers dry. We added claymore mines to the arsenal. These stand-alone, above-the-ground mines were built to explode away from the bunker. The explosives could be detonated by us while on watch. The only danger was if the enemy turned the mine toward the bunker and could get us to fire at ourselves. We also laid listening devices around the hillside. We couldn't go down as far as we needed because of the unmapped ARVN mines. The devices were so sensitive that a rat walking by sounded like an elephant charging! We had so many false alarms, that if a real VC probe took place, I am not so sure that any of us would have taken the warning seriously.

Notice the dust the chopper is making at the bottom of Hill 69 on one of its many supply runs. We are passing up boxes of c-rations, five gallon cans of water, and artillery ammunition.

I always considered Hill 69 to be one of the safest places during my almost ten months in Southeast Asia. According to Ken Sympson, on one of his tours on 69, a tunnel was discovered that connected to the village below. They could have poured hundreds of men in the middle of us before we could even react. I sure am glad I didn't know that. The tunnel was long and then straight up with bamboo ladders. The VC emptied the dug out dirt into a nearby stream. I grudgingly admired their engineers. With only rudimentary tools (picks and shovels), they could tunnel thousands of yards and be within a foot of their goal.

All the company radio operators pooled their tents and ponchos and fastened them to the permanent antenna at the apex of the hill. We had a huge tight teepee with an opening at the top. We rummaged around the trash dump on the northwest end of the hill and found sixty discarded, used, PRC radio batteries. The batteries were useless individually, but when wired together, they created a generator that could power a low-watt light bulb. We were able to run it at dusk and early in the morning, but not at dark because some of the light would filter out and the enemy could hone their guns in on us.

I learned much of what I was supposed to be doing with the radio on Hill 69. The other operators, including Fred Price, let me translate messages from Battalion and transmit them back. The code changed each day. On Monday it might be minus four. That meant if the letter "d" was used, it really was the fourth letter back which was "a." Each letter was transmitted by the corresponding word, for example, a was alpha, b was bravo, c was charlie, and so on. It took hours to write and send a daily order for supplies. All of that effort to be secretive, and all Charlie had to do was watch the helos land and surely he could figure out our strength. Actually things were so confining that most of us would have welcomed a fight with Victor Charlie.

Each night we stood watch. The damp weather and drizzling rain necessitated constant attention to our gear and rifles. After each heavy rain, the red mud became a sticky mess to walk in. As soon as the rain halted, everyone placed their stuff outside to dry and scraped the mud off boots, rifles, ponchos, sleeping bags, etc. Then the rains would reappear and the cycle started again. We were daily making trips to the bottom of the hill to help lug up the flown-in supplies. We pooled our c-rations and made helmets full of mulligan stew. The postage was free and we wrote to everybody we knew. Card games sprang up in almost every bunker. Our teepee was big and roomy and was everyone's favorite place to play. But everything got old, and the hill top seemed like a prison.

All night the artillery was constantly firing. Boom, Boom, Boom from dark to light. I did learn that man can get used to almost anything. When it was my time to sleep, not even the constant firing bothered me. I do think it affected my hearing, though. I was talking to one of the artillery officers recently. I told him I thought of him every Sunday morning at church. I can hear the music just fine, but the words to the hymns melt together and are hard to make out. All that noise he created on 69 finally caught up with me after I passed fifty!

Lt. Brown after a rain storm. Notice the caved-in bunker to his left and his mud-covered boots.

The mosquitoes were not much of a problem, but the rats were awful. The dump and toilet area were crawling with them. I really hated to sit on the two seater because of the rats below. We were all concerned that one would crawl into our sleeping bags and bite or scratch us. One night a rat the size of a cat climbed to the top of our teepee and slid down the other side. He was having such a good time, he did that over and over all night long. I can tolerate snakes, spiders and bugs, but I despise rats. Rotation day off 69 was very welcome.

Sometime during December the Marines at Chu Lai were treated to a show by Bob Hope. With Bob were Les Brown and his Band of Renown, Joey Heatherton, and a bunch of beautiful girls who had recently won various beauty contests. Bob's jokes were of the local area and always involved a serviceman. If I didn't know better, I would have sworn he was one of us. Looking back, I guess he was one of us because of all the good he brought to Chu Lai. Joey Heatherton was one of the most beautiful women I had ever seen. She had more energy than a full platoon of Marines. Her legs were shapely and long. When she danced and kicked her foot over her head, thousands of lonely Marines went absolutely wild! No one would believe me, but on her last number she pointed at me and smiled. Life just didn't get any better than mine in December of 1965!

At the show we all forgot that there was a war going on. Thousands of Marines were gathered around a hastily built stage that was located in a depression of sandy ground which resembled a bowl. Most of our officers were up front, especially the high-ranking ones. Ten well-placed mortar shells would have easily killed 500 men. I was glad the VC wasn't thinking what I was!

A few days before Christmas, our platoon sergeant told me he had one more slot for R&R and asked if I wanted it. The guys who had spent their R&R in Bangkok said the Thai women were the most beautiful in the world and also the most friendly. Sydney, Taipei, and even Saigon were great places to spend four days. I asked him about the destination and he replied, "Okinawa, and be ready tomorrow morning to leave if you want to go." I had already been to Okinawa, but I would at least get to spend the holidays out of Vietnam.

We landed at Kadenna Air Force base after many hours in a cold C-130 cargo plane. Our seats were racks along the walls with harness belts fastened around us (the cargo) to keep us from sliding all over the place. We were billeted in Camp Butler and had no responsibilities. We went to bed when we wanted, got up when we wanted, went where we wanted, ate what we wanted — just like being retired or on vacation. Much of my first day was spent in the rack. The exhaustion from all of those nights of getting little sleep and then going all day finally caught up with me. R&R means rest and relaxation, and I got plenty of both.

I was the only Echo member at Butler, but did meet some other R&R Marines to spend time with. We rented a taxi and rode all the way to the capital, Naha City. We stopped on the way back at Kadenna for lunch. I still couldn't believe how well the Air Force treated its men on Kadenna. Their PX had ten times what any of ours had. I found a telegraph office and sent a

Merry Christmas message to the folks. Outside the Kadenna gate I picked up a bottle of Chivas Regal scotch for Mr. Brown per his request. I had never heard of that kind of scotch, and for $13 it had to be something special.

My last night I got a steam bath and massage that was unforgettable. The owner of the massage parlor sent his teenage daughter in to give me a bath. She was about four-feet-eight inches and weighed at most seventy-five pounds. She was all business, and to make sure her mama san checked in on us every few minutes. The bath and steam shower soaked out all the impurities Vietnam had deposited over the last few months. My pores were squeaky clean from the alternating hot and cold showers. She then had me lie on my stomach and gave me a massage that included walking on my back with her tiny feet. After forty-five minutes my muscles were so relaxed, I could barely walk! My only regret was that I didn't do this the first night and each one there after.

After arriving back at Chu Lai, the first person I looked up was the Lt. I pulled out the bottle and proudly presented it to him. He wanted to know how much he owed me. "Thirteen dollars," I mumbled.

"Oh no, please don't tell me you paid more than $7?" he shockingly asked.

"Lt, this papa san outside Kadenna said that was the lowest price he would take." I went from a hero to a goat in a matter of moments! What a country bumpkin I was.

Recently, I was talking with Doc Martin, Third Platoon's corpsman. He asked me if I remembered the afternoon when a party of VC started firing into our compound. He said the Lt. had just come back from R&R and brought back a bottle of Chivas Regal. He shared it and emptied it with four guys in the CP tent. We were almost never attacked in daylight inside our inner perimeter, but were really taking some heavy small arms fire on this particular day. He said everyone was real glassy eyed, and Brown commented if this attack continued, the four of them weren't going to be of much help.

I interrupted and stated, "I was the one who brought that bottle back from R&R."

Then Martin said, "That's right and you overpaid for it, too!"

Thirty-six years later and that $13 is still a memory for too many people!

In January our battalion was removed from a lot of the perimeter duty and assigned to a group called Delta Force. General Walt, the commanding general of all the Marines in Vietnam, wanted more offense from his troops, and Delta Force would lead the way. Intelligence noted large units of Charlies were setting up operations in Southern I Corps. The strategy of exposing ourselves on open patrols to sniper fire and then turning on the shooter was "nickel and dime-ing" us to death, literally. We were losing men to land mines, booby traps, and small arms fire all the time. Occasionally we caught Charlie in groups of five to ten men, but normally they were being wasted one and two at a time. This was not typical of the way Marines were trained to fight. Delta Force would restore the aggression and attack mode the previous strategy had taken from us.

Doc Martin and Doc Collins were fearless and very competent corpsmen for Third Platoon.

Second Battalion was constantly getting replacements. I remember two guys in particular, Billy and William. The first time I saw them, they both had their skivvies dropped to the ankles and were bent over. About ten of us were gathered around laughing as Doc Martin gave them a shot of penicillin to knock out something they picked up on leave. Billy spoke very little but

William talked all the time. He said he was from Richmond, Virginia, and was twenty-three years old. He looked like Oil Can Harry with his thin mustache and slicked hair. He was wearing a gold Rolex watch and had on a huge diamond ring. He claimed to be a professional gambler and asked if there were any card games going on in our group. I told him a few of the guys played, but the stakes were small. Something told me to steer clear of this dude.

We were camped on the plains, a flat sandy area southwest of the air base, back behind the outer lines. While the brass was in the planning stages of our offensive operations, we would go on long patrols and search the villages for any sign of the enemy. We were going out four or five miles in front of the outer lines. We were sitting ducks, daring the enemy to expose himself by firing at us. The radio was heavy in addition to my regular gear, but in a strange sort of way I felt it offered me protection from being shot. The platoon commander and the radioman were the two guys the enemy wanted to eliminate the most. Cut off the head and eliminate the ability to communicate and the platoon would be more vulnerable. The VC were terrible shooters, and their weapons seemed to always be dirty and rusty. Lt Brown and I thought if they aimed at us, the odds of them hitting something else was almost a sure thing. Now, thirty-six years later, that makes no sense at all. If they shoot enough times, the odds of a lucky shot hitting its target…

After a long time out in the boondocks, camp was mighty good. Hot meals and showers were free. If they charged for them, all of us would have spent everything we had for those luxuries. On the plains, which were called The Catfishes after our Battalion Commander Lt. Colonel Bull Fisher, we lived in large tents and slept on cots instead of the ground. Camp time lasted two or three days before we had to go back out. There were plenty of card games and few work details. Everyone seemed to want me in their game. The word around was I had plenty of money, and was so lucky the luck had to run out soon. I did have a pocket full of cash. My system worked like a charm. I remember losing a hand here and there, but rarely did I lose a game of 500 gin rummy. In poker I learned it was easier to bluff when you had plenty of dollars. I took so many pots with nothing but a straight face. Each time my pockets started to bulge out, I bought a money order and mailed it home. In January and February I sent $1400 home on a lance corporal's pay of less than $150 a month, which included $55 in combat pay.

William, the gambler from Richmond, and I started playing gin rummy one afternoon. I knew better than to play poker with him. I really believed

106

him about his being a professional by the way he could shuffle and deal. We played every chance we could for the next couple of days. I finally won all of his money. He became obsessed with playing me. After each losing hand he would say, "I know you're cheating and I'm watching you closely. Tell me how you're doing it and I promise I won't get mad."

After denying I was cheating, and with macho bravado, I warned him, "Don't you ever accuse me of being a cheater again!"

We then started playing again. He put up his watch and ring as collateral for a loan. William was addicted to finding out how I was beating him. He was willing to pay almost anything to find out.

I was halfway to wearing a real Rolex watch when he snapped. His patience had worn out. He picked up his M14 and released the safety lock and put the barrel in my face. He screamed, "Nobody cheats me. I don't care if they burn me, you ain't cheating me!" This man was crazy mad, and his glazed look told me he meant business.

I put my palms out slowly and promised that I had never cheated him. I said calmly, "I don't have any use for a diamond ring, and I don't want your watch either. Look, put the safety back on and get that out of my face, now!" I don't know what made me say that, except I thought I'd have a better chance at reasoning with him if I didn't grovel.

Miraculously, he lowered the rifle and I left the tent shaking from head to toe. The closest I had come to dying in Vietnam was not from a booby trap, a mortar shell explosion, a helicopter crash, or an AK47 bullet, but an M14 round from a fellow Marine. Whew!!

Toward the end of January, Marine Corps Command in Da Nang, came up with Delta Force's first large offensive operation. Intelligence reported that as many as three Viet Cong Regiments were operating out of the South I Corps area. The Army 1st Calvary and two ARVN divisions were going to sweep the Viet Cong out of II Corps into where we would be. They named the operation Double Eagle. It was supposed to include the largest amphibious landing since Inchon during the Korean War. Everyone prepared for a bigger operation than Starlite.

Echo Company was chosen to go in ahead of the other members of Delta Force. We had the responsibility of capturing a cliff top that controlled the beach landing zone. The planners gave us only one day to accomplish the objective. Many battalions would make amphibious landings the following day. The beach was called Red Beach. We had to make sure the name wasn't for Marine blood spilled there.

We are waiting for the helicopters to arrive. In the foreground from the left are me, Lt. Brown, Doc Collins sitting on a water can, and Staff Sgt. Neal who was our platoon sergeant. At our reunion on April 6, 2002, Mr. Brown asked me if he ever fussed at me. I told him only once and it was over my grimy cover (hat). After looking at my dirty cover, he had plenty of justification.

The 34s heloed us to a spot about six miles from the cliff top. It was a well-fortified ARVN outpost that had tanks and some heavy artillery within its compound. In the early morning we headed for the beach and then on to our objective. The first mile was possibly the roughest terrain any of us had ever navigated. We were being fired on constantly. My good friend John Hollars killed the first VC of the operation there. Ted Gray's squad had seven confirmed VC kills before daylight. The incoming rounds were coming from an identifiable village; however, the task of securing the high ground quickly would not allow us to pursue Charlie beyond 200 yards from the main unit. We were disappointed, but understood. It took us at least five hours to get everyone through all the jagged rocks and thick underbrush. The next four miles almost wiped out every member of the force. We were on the beach in soft sand, carrying extra gear, in heavy boots, and exhausted from the first mile's march. Major Defazio, an older WWII veteran, was in charge of the group and pushed us because we were behind schedule and the mission was so vital.

When the company finally arrived at the base of the cliff, our thighs and calves were cramping and most thought this was as far as they could go. The average weight we were carrying was seventy-five pounds. We had not been resupplied since landing. Everybody was out of water, and many were getting dehydrated. The column was stretched out behind me for maybe a half mile. When we arrived at the base of the cliff, I just fell backwards into the sand. I thought this would be a good time to rest and wait on everyone to catch up. Lt. Brown went over to an air wing radioman and picked up his PRC-47 and told us we had to get to the top and then rest. Up the side of the cliff he went, carrying a radio that outweighed mine by twenty pounds.

Lt. looked back at all the lethargic Marines and yelled for us to follow him. His tone meant right that minute! The steep incline was 162 meters from the base and at first glance looked to be impossible to climb. I thought to myself, *I'm not letting an old married man (Brown was twenty-five) out do me.* I got up and started climbing. We matched each other step for step. Both of us (me more so) were grunting, groaning, cramping, and operating on empty. Finally we made it to the top, totally wiped out. Both of us fell on our backs and tried to regain our breath and composure.

All of a sudden we both realized that we might have company. We walked over about forty feet from where we had dropped and found the deepest foxholes I had ever seen. We must have surprised Charlie because he left in such a hurry. They only took their weapons with them and left all their food stuff behind. If we hadn't been so exhausted and fallen on our backs, possibly we could have captured or killed some of the escaping soldiers.

The next day we watched two Marine battalions land on Red Beach. From our position on the cliff top, an enemy 155 howitzer could have inflicted heavy casualties on the Marines below. It was easy to understand why the Delta planners had us secure the cliff top before commencing the attack. Phantom fighter jets were all over the sky that day. We got quite a show from our ringside seats.

The following morning, Echo eased down the cliff side and headed for another area a few miles away. There were two Navy Seabees trapped, taking heavy ground fire. We never learned why they were out by themselves surveying in an area known to be enemy territory. Battalion asked us to rescue them since they were on our way. On our way? It took a whole day to get them out of harm's way.

The Company had to wade across a wide, fairly deep river to get to them. On the other side we started taking lots of AK47 fire from the side of a rocky mountain. The Phantom jets were called in from Chu Lai to blast the ambushers from their holes. The flyboys reported heavy gunfire every time they flew over the area. As soon as the planes finished firing, the VC would race out of their hiding places and let go with a steady stream of tracers. Finally we (and the jets) silenced the aggressors. In the meantime, PFC Imel raced across open fields under extreme fire and brought back the Seabees. He was awarded a medal for his heroism.

On the way back down to the river, someone threw a hand grenade at some movement in thick underbrush. A mad, excited water buffalo charged out toward one of Second Platoons' squads. I believe when everything was said and done, the buffalo had to be killed and at least two of our men had broken bones. Sometime later, Corpsman Zimmerman, in his brand-new utilities, was standing between Ed Brummett and another dirty Marine. A VC spotted the three and fired at the tall Doc, probably thinking he was someone important with his medical pouch and dark green utilities. Doc was hit in the lower back and immediately screamed, "That little SOB, that little SOB shot me, I can't believe that SOB shot me!" He must have hollered that twenty times. We realized he was in a lot of pain and being shot was serious business, but he absolutely cracked everybody up.

Some guys saw the VC duck into a rocky hole and rushed to the spot. A sergeant pulled back a tree branch and exposed a deep cave that housed the shooter. He wouldn't come up when ordered, so one of the squad members dropped a grenade down the hole while the Sgt. held the branch back. Just as the grenade was dropped the branch slipped out of his hand. The branch threw the young Private over the opening just as the grenade exploded! His flak jacket was blown to pieces, but the only place he was actually hurt was his feelings. He did however have some choice words for his squad leader.

We set up a machine gun on our side of the river to cover the crossing, leaving Sgt. Brummett in charge of the rear. The water was up to my chin and over many of the guys' heads. When most of us had crossed, another machine gun was set up to cover the remaining men on the other side. As Brummett stepped into the water, Charlie opened up with everything he had.

With water spraying all over, the taller guys held onto the smaller Marines and they all made it safely to the bank. What a day that was!

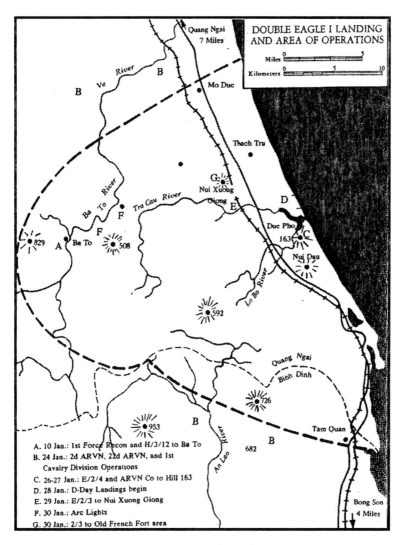

Echo Company was chosen to lead the Delta Force operation named Double Eagle and secure a vital cliff, which overlooked the largest amphibious landing since the Korean War at Inchon. After action map was prepared by Jack Shulinson, U S Marines in Vietnam .

Double Eagle lasted well into February. Delta Force killed over 350 VC, but most of the enemy had run away when they saw what we were doing. Charlie ran south into II Corps where the 1st Calvary and two ARVN divisions were supposed to be driving them into us. I understood almost 2,000 VC lost their lives in II Corps escaping from us.

One of the best moments of the operation happened on the final day. There were not enough choppers to fly all of us back to Chu Lai. We boarded a troop ship for the ride home. The Navy laundered our grungy clothes, fed us three outstanding meals, provided steaming hot showers, and bunks with clean sheets. What a life those sailors lived! All of them treated us like we were something special.

The next month was spent on some long search and destroy missions around the base. We were going out many times with the local Vietnamese militia on forays into the countryside. Those men who were called PFs were better fighters than the ARVN. This particular group was responsible for the protection of the villages around Chu Lai. Their leader was a tough little hombre by the name of Captain Noto. He had a pencil-thin mustache and also looked like a slant-eyed version of Oil Can Harry. I believe he hated the VC even more than we did. Many times when we questioned the villagers, they might fear the VC so much that they would lie about what they knew. Not so when we had the militia leader with us. I think they feared what he would do to them if he even thought they were lying, more so than what the VC would do. One day we witnessed him hitting an old mama san in the face with his rifle butt. No one ever trusted him after that. The man was plain mean.

The militia leader had another responsibility . He and the village chiefs protected the virtue of the village girls. The rural village girls around our area were nothing like the city dwellers in Saigon, Da Nang, and Hue. These girls would not let their eyes meet ours, they were modest, and the last thing they wanted was to be with one of us. One Marine on patrol gave a cute teenager a $3 watch he had won in a PX contest. He had another watch and just wanted to be nice. The village chief found out about the gift, and thought it was too expensive to not expect anything in return. He beat the girl black and blue. Their morals were so much higher than ours. We really had to be careful, even with normal American flirting. A relationship with one of us would have been an automatic death sentence for the girl if found out.

We spent quite a few nights in militia leader Noto's village. Actually, at times we used it as a base from which to patrol. The village was quite large

*The Vietnamese with the map to Lt. Brown's left is the notorious
Popular Forces commander, Captain Noto.*

and well fortified. One afternoon a few of us ordered an egg omelette meal
full of onions from an enterprising mama san. Man, was that meal tasty after
days of c-rations. It only cost fifty cents.

That night all of the radio operators camped together and shared the watch
with the captain's operator. On my hour and a half watch something grabbed
the inside of my lower stomach. It felt like battery acid that would explode at
any second. I ran for the two seater the Marines had built for the village and
barely made it. I was gone no more than ten minutes. The Captain picked the
wrong time to walk by the radio tent. I had left the radio on and there were
four Marines close by, but they were asleep. My explanation must have been
believable because I was never written up. I stuck to either the mess tent or c-
rations after that.

On our trips out into the boondocks, we not only were trying to search
and destroy, but we were there to uplift and make friends. Our constant show
of force gave the villagers a sense of security. The corpsmen were always

patching up the locals, and if they couldn't fix the malady, arrangements were made to have a base doctor look at their problem. The kids were so easy to make smile. A pack of crackers, gum, or a candy bar brought more happiness than if one gave an American kid a bicycle. Those people were desperate for anything. The poverty was everywhere. As poor as the people were, the VC would come at night and take their meager baskets of rice and leave them to go hungry. The South Vietnamese people didn't have a chance.

One day I was out with Sgt. Wilson's squad. If we were not in platoon formation I assumed the duty of what I was trained to be — a rifleman. The squad was crossing an open area of rice paddies. There were clumps of trees and bushes dotting the area. All of a sudden, from about 100 yards to our left front, three or four AK47s started firing. Wilson yelled for me to take my team (William and Billy) over to the VC flank and lay down some fire. His orders were for the three of us to race across an open field to a brush covering and open fire.

William said, "I ain't runnin' over there and gettin' killed!"

"Me neither," said Billy.

I pointed my rifle in William's face and said excitedly, "You can race over to those bushes with me and probably live, or you can die here for sure for disobeying a direct order!"

Both got up and helped flush out the enemy. Was I bluffing? Did I remember the time when William pointed his rifle in my face and did that influence me? I don't know, everything happened so fast, but I think I was bluffing. I don't believe I could live with myself if I had shot another Marine. I am just thankful he didn't challenge me. Neither one of us ever mentioned that episode to anyone.

My most frustrating time in Nam was on another squad-size patrol. It was late afternoon and we were heading back to camp. Our point spotted nineteen black-pajama-clad, straw-hatted men with rifles at their side. They were running at a steady pace and were about eight hundred yards in front of us. We were catching up with them when somebody determined we were close to First Battalion's area of responsibility. We didn't want to get shot by our own troops so we radioed for permission to cross their lines. Sometime back, we did not get permission to cross into another battalion's area and a helicopter strafed us. It took almost an hour for the First Battalion's Colonel to relay permission back to us to cross. Nineteen Charlies escaped to fight another day. I have often wondered if any of those nineteen put a name on the Wall. Where the heck was that Colonel?!!

I never asked myself why I was in Vietnam, or if it was the right thing. I had never seen people in so much need. Their life span was 60% of ours. The men, and especially the women, appeared as if they were in their sixties when they actually were in their thirties. Life was so hard and survival was measured by the day. Their schools and clinics were destroyed. The babies were filthy and were lucky to make it to the age of five. Most didn't. They just needed help, and the enemy did everything it could to intimidate and hurt those innocent people.

One incident out of hundreds stands out in my memory. This small village with maybe three babies under the age of two had one cow. We found her one day still standing after taking nine rounds in her body from a VC raid the night before. The only source of calcium and nourishment for those babies would be dead in a little while. For no reason other than intimidation, those cruel and heartless monsters had sentenced three babies to the beginning of malnutrition and possibly death. I didn't understand the politics of the war in 1966. All I really knew was that communism was wrong, most of the people didn't want it, and they deserved much better. When I question the right or wrong of being there, I see the faces of those three filthy, little, doomed babies and know for me I was in the right place.

Over the past 35 years, the Vietnam veteran has really taken a hit over his involvement in the war. Our Country asked much of Her young servicemen in the '60s and early part of the '70s. We were asked to spend 13 months away from home in a place that was anything but hospitable. We were asked to fight a war without the full support of those back home. We were asked to fight a competent, determined enemy with one hand, and sometimes two, tied behind our backs. In my opinion, the restrictions placed on us by the politicians doomed the outcome of the war and cost the lives of thousands of America's fighting men. We were asked to risk our lives and almost 60,000 laid down their lives. Knowledgeable historians will record that the Vietnam vet did everything asked of him and then some. We won every battle and yet many label us as the first Americans to lose a war. We've heard over and over that Vietnam was the wrong war at the wrong time in the wrong place. Many point out that all the sacrifices we made there were pointless and have served no purpose.

I had the honor of speaking with former Commandant of the Marine Corps, P. X. Kelley in September of 2002, about the perception many hold of Vietnam. General Kelley gave me permission to include a conversation he had with President Reagan about the President's view of the Vietnam veteran. They were alone on the tarmac at Andrews Air Force Base and had been in a lengthy discussion about the war. The President opined, "You know, P. X., while in the minds of many Americans, Vietnam was an unpopular war, it proved to the world the depth of our resolve against communism. For political reasons at home, we were forced to withdraw our forces, but for six long years the Russians and the whole world witnessed an impressive demonstration of our combat capabilities. **I am convinced that the Vietnam War was the main reason the Cold War ended.**"

I believe that most every person who experienced a sacrifice, whether it be losing a child, brother, parent, relative or friend, for those that sustained horrible injuries, and even for those who gave their lives, would agree that to diminish communism to irrelevancy was worth the price.

Chapter Nine

Operation Texas

On March 17, 1966, Third Platoon was out on another search and destroy mission to the west of the air base. Intelligence passed down word that Charlie might try some hit and run that night on an area for which we were responsible. At dusk, Lt. Brown sent out a squad of Marines to set up a fifty-foot-long ambush. The site was at the base of a small hill and was at an intersection of two popular paths. The location he chose was perfect, except for one small detail. On the other side of the path was a huge field of rice paddies which was a breeding ground for the largest and most aggressive mosquitoes I had ever seen.

The sun had already dropped to the bottom of the sky. There was just a small amount of light left when we found the site. The tall elephant grass provided excellent camouflage. The night was calm and still, which was not good. Any breeze at all would keep flying bugs at bay. Before we left camp, all of us decided to go easy on the mosquito repellent. The strong perfume smell might give our position away. We spread out, got comfortable, unlaced our boots, and quietly waited for Charlie. He decided to stay home on this particular night. The only enemy encountered that night was a swarm of giant mosquitoes. What a problem! Many were the size of silver dollars and they feasted on us. I had bite marks from head to toe. The marks were especially bad on the tops of my feet and between my toes. There was no way we could have surprised anybody that night with all the groaning, squirming, and smacking.

The next morning, we limped back into camp. The squad leader reported the only action encountered were some Viet Cong mosquitoes. Corporal Kemp said, "We killed plenty of them, but they might have gotten the best of us." That was the only battle Third Platoon ever lost. Everybody had experienced something like that before, but not as severe. Usually the bite mark welts would go away if we wouldn't scratch too much.

Corporal Kemp is disarming a 82 mm booby trap with Lt. Brown giving moral support. I asked respectfully, "Lt., why are you up here?" He replied, "I won't ask any of my men to do something I wouldn't do."

The next day the platoon headed back to camp. It took two days of leisurely marching to get there. Along the way we searched a bunch of small villages. In each one, there were always natives who had problems that our two docs could help. In one village I got a shave the old-fashioned way — with a straight razor. While the villager was shaving the fuzz along my chin and neck, the thought occurred to me that this man might be a VC. When he scraped the razor along my Adam's Apple, I really tightened up. There were five Marines waiting their turn, and I figured there was no way he would cut my throat with them that close. Some of the guys were eating food offered to them, but not me. I would have turned down pecan pie after the cramps and diarrhea I had recently experienced from one of the local cooks.

The Lt. had us march through the paddies instead of marching on the paths, more so on this trip home. Charlie was laying more booby traps, and they were becoming more sophisticated and deadlier. We rarely saw the crude ones, such as pungi sticks dipped in human or animal waste anymore. A particular mine that was becoming popular was one that detonated by tripping a wire. The mine would pop up about three feet high and explode, inflicting terrible injuries. Most of the mines were placed in well-traveled areas and somehow the locals knew to avoid those places. Many times they would point out the location of the mines to us. However, if the VC found out a villager helped us destroy one of their mines, the villager and/or his chief's head would be removed.

I am eating a can of ham and lima beans with my shirt off. Notice I have removed my boots to dry out my feet and socks. Almost every time we stopped, I needed to take care of my infected feet.

The rice fields were a deep green color, indicating an abundance of human and animal fertilizer had been applied. On the night of the 19th, I pulled my socks off and noticed plenty of infected bite marks. I knew my feet had been itching, but never dreamed they looked that bad. The welts above my knees were healing up, but where I had been in the filthy water, the marks didn't look good. I changed socks that night, but had to sleep with my wet boots laced up because of the mosquitoes. The next day was more of the same. That day we added two stream crossings where the water was neck deep and full of leeches. When I pulled off my boots to search for the leeches I noticed the welts had turned into blisters with pus in them. We got into camp around dark and I was limping pretty badly by then. I washed up and slept barefoot under a mosquito netting, hoping the open air would be good medicine.

The following morning in the daylight I saw that the blisters and bite marks were infected and my skin color was pink below my knees. I ate breakfast and found platoon corpsman Jerry Collins. After looking at my feet, he sent me to the battalion aid station. The doctor examined my feet and gave me a bar of antiseptic drying soap to use three times per day. I was also instructed to wear shower flip flops for three days. I received a light-duty slip and was told to revisit the aid station on the 23rd. Our platoon was scheduled for some well-deserved rest for the next few days. Having the light-duty slip guaranteed that I would escape any work details, and I looked forward to the rest. I noticed at supper that I wasn't the only one there wearing flip flops. The mess tent was full. All four of the battalion's companies were in camp and it took forever to get through the chow line. The meal was worth the wait. We had Southern fried chicken with thick crust, mashed potatoes, green beans, rolls, and sheet cake. I can barely remember things that happened yesterday, yet I remember what we had for supper on March 20, 1966. That has to be another sign of advanced aging.

Around 2000 hours, we were told that tomorrow, 2nd Battalion was going to war. The name of the battle would be Operation Texas. We had a new Battalion Commander, Lt. Col. P.X. Kelley, and he was special. Colonel Kelley would visit the front lines at night without wearing a pistol. He seemed to enjoy telling us, as long as we were on the front line, the enemy had no chance of breaking through to him, which eliminated his need for a side arm. Col. Kelley thought there was a good possibility of us killing a bunch of enemy gooks south of Quang Ngai City, which was south of Chu Lai. Fox Company would fly out first and then us. We were to land before noon in the Vin Tuy valley close to some villages called the Phuong Dinh Complex. My old outfit, Third Battalion, Seventh Marines, had already landed in the northwestern part of the valley. They were supposed to hook up with us, and together we would drive the enemy into the South China Sea.

I didn't give staying back in camp much thought. I had an excuse from the doctor, but what if my friends got into trouble? Who would man the radio? By now I felt very responsible and indispensable about my position as platoon radioman. The fact was, most of the guys could handle the radio, but because it weighed so much, they wanted me to carry it. How could I face the guys who would come back? How could I face myself? Would I tell them I stayed behind because I had some mosquito bites on my feet? I think another compelling reason to go was the opportunity to kill Viet Cong. I was beginning to have a real dislike for our opponent. I crawled onto my cot and pulled the mosquito net over me and slept like a baby. That would be the last good night's sleep I would enjoy for a long time.

The next morning we packed, ate a hearty breakfast, and walked to the helicopter landing zone. The choppers had already taken Fox Company to the valley and were returning to pick us up. They were on time, and after a long flight, landed us in an open field west of an uneventful-looking village. There was the noise of small arms fire in the background, but that didn't concern any of us. It never dawned on us that this place would soon turn into a horrible killing field for them and for us.

We assembled just east of the landing zone and unloaded our packs. The area looked like south Georgia with the exception of the rice paddies. There were tall pine trees, eight to ten feet apart, planted in red sandy soil. This wooded area was about ten acres and had an open field running north to south, splitting the woods. There was a deep ditch in the field about two hundred yards to our front.

We were thirty minutes away from battle. Echo Company was chosen to lead a frontal assault on the village east of the ditch. We were waiting on the A-4s flying overhead to drop some napalm on the ditch in front of us, just in case the VC were dug in there. I leaned back against a tree and lit a cigarette. Out of the corner of my eye I saw movement in the trees across the ditch. Others saw the same thing because everybody started pulling off rounds. After a few minutes we stopped firing and they stopped moving.

Fox Company started walking single file through our lines. They were headed to a position southwest of the village and were going to support our assault by laying down supporting fire. A Fox squad leader yelled, "Randy, is that you?" It was John Boren. We hadn't seen each other in ten months. He had been over since November 1965, and transferred to Fox only recently. I wished that we hadn't been split up back at Camp Pendleton. John would have never let me binge drink like I did in Olongapo.

The A-4 Skyhawks swooped down and dropped two napalm bombs. The gasoline-soaked jelly barrels hit the ditch perfectly. We could see the canisters tumble to the ground, then bounce forward and explode. The fire shot up at least two hundred feet above the tree line. For a moment I actually felt sorry for anyone caught in that inferno. There was no way anybody could survive that torching. I figured the Marine Air Wing had just eliminated the need for the grunts to do battle there. We probably would do a body count mission on all of those incinerated Charlies and go back to the base tonight. Was I ever wrong! John told me years later the enemy had dug deep foxholes. The holes were actually traps and had a lid on top. They were expecting the napalm and just closed their trap doors when it came.

These were not normal guerilla fighters. They were troops from North Vietnam (NVA) and were some of the enemy's best soldiers. Their engineers were also very good. They not only had one trench, but three for us to cross. Their concertina wire and bunkers were well camouflaged and excellently placed to inflict maximum casualties. There were deep tunnels to bring reinforcements into the battle. The tunnels were also escape routes if necessary. This place was unlike anything we had ever seen. Actually, the enemy had been preparing this site since 1954 and used it as a regional headquarters to control a large area of countryside.

Lt. Brown came by and told us we had about ten minutes before we would move out. I lit another cigarette and stood up. For some reason my grandfather's face popped up in front of me. He was such a good storyteller and could hold my attention for hours. I thought, *What if when I get back home, I tell Daddy Black that during a battle I repeated the 23rd Psalm?*

Great idea, and the last thing I wanted to lie about was the Bible, so I recited as much of the chapter as I could remember. "Yea thou I walk through the valley of the shadow of death I will fear no evil, for thou art with me," was all I could come up with. I was so pleased with myself for thinking of this story to tell him. He would be very proud of me, I thought.

I walked over to Gafkowski and told him where my radio code books were, and if something were to happen to me to be sure and not let them be captured. The book contained hundreds of code words that meant something else, such as "Ford" meant wounded and "Cadillac" meant killed. The enemy monitored our transmissions and I didn't want them to have my book. I told him that there was not a chance that I would be hurt, but just in case. That was the only time I ever had a negative premonition about something happening.

I put on my gear and strapped on the PRC 10 and made a test call. I slung the rifle over my shoulder and walked over to where Lt. Brown stood. He had the platoon on line in front of the trees facing the burned-out ditch. This open area was once a rice paddy, but now was dry land. Lt. Brown decided that our position (I was never over five feet away from him) should be on top of an old dike. It was two feet higher, and from there he would have better control of the platoon; the men could more easily see him, he could better make out the location of Charlie, but the enemy could also see us with little trouble.

As we were waiting for the Colonel to give the go ahead to start the assault, helicopters were flying over the village and were reporting little movement down below. I was absolutely unafraid. I knew that they would be shooting at the two of us and it was certain they would miss. After all, I was a nineteen-year-old Marine lance corporal who was invincible.

Lt. yelled, " Move it out!"

We slowly but methodically moved toward the ditch line that had to be barren from the napalm drops. We had moved about fifteen feet when one of the low-flying helicopter pilots radioed the command post, "Colonel, my God, they are coming out of the holes, huts, trenches! There are hundreds of them everywhere!"

It was too late to stop us and let the artillery section soften them up. Echo was in front of the battalion in the lead assault position. We had 157 men and were going to face as many as 1500 of North Vietnam's best in a matter of seconds.

We moved fifteen more feet when war broke out. Mortars started firing, two machine guns opened up from our left and right flank, and enemy soldiers in helmets and uniforms (I had never seen a VC in anything other than black pajamas) started popping out of spider holes and firing AK47s at close range.

Lt. Brown was unshakable under fire. He showed absolutely no fear. I think he felt like I did, that he also was invincible. Our men started bunching up on the platoon's right. Lt. screamed over the deafening explosions for the men to spread it out. He extended his right arm toward the offending parties in order to make a point. My face followed his outstretched hand to see who was getting too close to one another.

Directly to our front at about eleven o'clock, at close range, two NVAs sprang from a well concealed set of spider holes. They opened up on us with their AK 47s. Lt. saw them emerge from their hiding places but had his shooting hand stretched out. By the time he pulled it down, the soldier on the left had fired a shot at us. Before he could fire another shot, Lt. blew him to kingdom come. The shooter on his right fired four shots into Lt. Brown. One round found the Lt.'s left forearm and the other three lodged in his pack. His arm was hurt badly and was bleeding profusely. Doc Martin ran to him and told him to wrap his belt around the arm and try to stop the bleeding. Doc said, "Lt., there are so many men hurt worse than you, I just can't spend anymore time with you, sir." Lt. Brown assured him that he understood.

I was one of those who was hurt worse. The NVA on the left had fired only one shot, thanks to Lt. Brown, but that shot hit me in the left front of my neck. The jolt caused me to pitch my rifle forward. Lt. grabbed the stock and in one motion pointed the barrel and fired at the VC who had just shot me. The shot was true and instantly killed the soldier. If he had been allowed to fire another shot, it probably would have hit me in the face. I never saw the man who shot me because I was looking to my right to see who was bunched up. At the bullet's impact, the jolt was the hardest hit I had ever taken. My Uncle Ira had a mule that couldn't be stalled in the barn because he kicked so hard that the stall boards would be smashed. That AK47 round felt like that mule kick.

A black fog covered me all over. It was like being knocked out and seeing stars, only there was no light whatsoever. From the top of the dike I started to float through the air in slow motion. I was never more frightened at anytime of my life than at that moment. I was going to die, or worse I was already dead. My first thought was that I had used up all of my chances to be right with God. I was slowly floating toward hell because that's where I thought I deserved to be. In desperation, I silently screamed, *Please God, don't let my mama go through burying me! She won't be able to handle that. Please save my soul.* A few moments later I hit the ground very hard. Stunned, I looked up into the beautiful blue sky and knew that I had just received two miracles from heaven. I was alive and my soul was saved!

I was lying on top of the big radio on my back with a feeling of peace that was beyond understanding. All the guilt I had been carrying had been taken away. I couldn't get up, maybe I was just stunned, I decided. I couldn't feel my feet or legs. My arms and body wouldn't respond to my commands to move. I tried to breathe and could not. When I crashed into the dry rice paddy, the jolt sent my knees into my face. My solar plexus was being squeezed so tightly I couldn't suck any air into my lungs. I never panicked. I looked up and calmly said, "God, I need my hands so I can breathe, please let me have them." Like air rushing out of a balloon, feeling exploded into my hands! I immediately threw my legs off my chest and took a deep breath of air. Battle was taking place all around me, but I don't remember any noise. It was so peaceful and quiet. Most people go through their whole life without experiencing a miracle; on March 21, 1966, I received three.

A little while later Doc Martin ran to where I was lying. He examined the entry wound and asked if I could move. I told him I could not but that I felt no pain. Lt. yelled for some men to get me out of there quickly and put me behind a dike about ninety feet from our position. Doc and a Marine picked me up and ran to the dike. They placed me gently on the ground and elevated my feet on top of the mound. They thought I was safe and left to go back to the front. Ray Wyatt was sent to retrieve my PRC10. It was shot to pieces. Lt. Brown saved my life twice that day. If he had not had me moved, I would have been the one shot to pieces.

I don't remember how long I laid there. Battle was taking place all around. Third Platoon was taking the brunt of the enemies' attention. The NVA had been waiting since 1954 when the French left for the Good Guys to visit their home. They unleashed a stifling amount of firepower on us. Our men returned an equal amount of ordinance on the VC, but soon were running low on ammo. Thomas Hood, our M79 man, was one of many chosen to locate more ammunition. In his search, Tom saw my boots on top of the dike. He said, "I thought the two boots looked like a periscope. I also saw that the VC were firing at them." He decided to investigate and found me behind the dike. He pulled my feet off the dike and brushed the sand the enemy rounds had been spraying out of my eyes.

With Tom's help, I now was sitting up half way with my back against the two to three foot high dry rice paddy dike. There was a tree a few feet away that provided a lot of dark shade. The young man with me would not leave my side. He stayed completely in control in the midst of all the noise and action around us. He convinced me nothing was wrong and we were perfectly safe. The only weapons we had were the empty shotgun-like M79 which fired 40mm grenades, and a side arm the young Marine carried. All this guy wanted to talk about was how fortunate I was. Morristown, Tennessee, would be my next stop and he kept repeating how lucky I was. He opened my pack of Winstons and wanted to know if he could light me a smoke. I thanked him but told him I had quit smoking. I made up my mind this time I really would keep my word.

I don't remember how much time passed until some members of Second Platoon came forward. First and Third Platoons led the first assault with Second in reserve. This was classic Marine Corps tactics. In the rare event the enemy broke through a gap in the line, there was another line of Leathernecks to fight and plug the hole. Second started removing the other two platoons' dead and injured back to the LZ. Four guys ran over to me, unrolled a poncho, and rolled me onto it. They were pleasant, but in a hurry and were rough with me. I weighed almost 190 lbs and they dragged me about a fourth of the way. I never realized it at the time, but we were still on the battlefield and Charlie still wanted to kill us.

We left the dry area and they started wading in the wet part of the field. Walking or running in that muck was difficult enough, but carrying a big Marine and at the same time receiving incoming rounds required nothing short of super human ability. Not until I wrote this paragraph did I realize the risk those four took in transporting me to the Landing Zone. Admiral Chester Nimitz once said of another era of Marines, "Uncommon valor was a common virtue." That quote is appropriate for those nameless Marines who rescued not only me but many others that day. Many gave their lives trying to bring their brothers back to safety. The greatest Man once said, "There is no greater love than the love that would cause a man to lay down his life for a friend." Semper Fi to all of you great warriors of Echo Company, Second Battalion, Fourth Marines!

On arriving at the LZ, a corpsmen directed the four to place me on a green canvas stretcher. I was quickly examined and reported that I was not in any pain. I could feel from two inches above my nipples and had the use of all my fingers except the little ones. My neck wound was bandaged and because there was no exit wound they determined the bullet was still in me someplace. The sun was shining overhead, but somebody stood by me and shaded me with his torso.

I didn't lie there very long until a helicopter landed to take me to Chu Lai. As they were about to load me, Lt. Brown ran over to me. He looked awful. His arm was in a dirty white gauze like sling and his face was white from all the blood he had lost. He leaned down to me and assured me everything would be all right. He told me to take care of myself and hoped to see me again soon. I said, "Thank you, sir," and smiled. After he left I wondered why I didn't tell him how much I admired him and wanted some day to be like him. Why didn't I thank him for the example he lived before us and the numerous times his leadership had saved our lives? I didn't know he had just saved my life twice. Hopefully, my smile told him how I really felt.

I learned later why Gary Brown looked so pale. After being shot in the right forearm, he tightly wrapped his shattered arm with his web belt and stopped much of the bleeding. Echo Company commander was out of action and Lt. was next in command. He turned over what remained of Third Platoon to the highest-ranking NCO left. That was Corporal Kemp who would do such a great job that Gen. Walt promoted him to staff sergeant and presented him with the nation's second-highest award, the Navy Cross. Lt. led two more assaults on the Viet Cong stronghold as the company commander. After the last skirmish, Colonel Kelley summoned his commanders to the rear for more instructions. This was when Lt. said goodbye to me. The Battalion Commander wanted one more charge into the village. The company leaders were headed back to their respective companies when Col. Kelley yelled, "Lt., where do you think you are going?"

Lt. Brown turned and wanted to say "I'm going back to Echo to prepare them for the attack," but instead lost consciousness and fell to the ground from the loss of blood. Col. Kelley got on the PRC 25 radio and summoned a Huey down to take Lt. Brown to the hospital in Chu Lai.

The unconscious Brown was placed in the bird and had his wounds attended shortly thereafter at Chu Lai. He would spend the next six weeks in various Navy hospitals, the last being at Jacksonville, Florida. He recovered the use of most of his arm and hand. Gary Brown won the Silver Star on that day for bravery, courage, and leadership above and beyond the call of duty. The next time I would see Gary was thirty-six years later. I learned he was still married to the same lady we talked about in Vietnam. He is a grandfather and father of two very successful children. He stayed in the Corps and served another tour of duty in Vietnam. He also served in the Persian Gulf War. He retired after thirty-two years of valuable service to his country, achieving the rank of Brigadier General. One of my greatest honors in life was serving with Gary Brown.

It took thirty-six years for me to realize many of the details of that day. My mom kept a scrapbook of my life and gave it to me the summer of 2002. I had no idea of its existence. In it was the telegram she received notifying my family that I was wounded. Also there were many articles about Operation Texas. The reports told about the battle and what a great victory it was for us.

I also met John Boren in October 2001 for the first time since 3-21-66. He told me about all the graves they found after the battle and that one had a

Viet Cong general buried in it. General Westmoreland, the leader of all American forces in Vietnam, could not believe that we had killed so many of North Vietnam's finest, so he flew to the battlefield to see for himself. John said the General assembled the Marines together and told them they were his best fighting force in Vietnam.

In the last year I have spoken to many comrades who were there — Ted Gray, TC Gardner, Chester Gafkowski, Ray Wyatt, Ken Sympson, Ed Martin, John Hollars, Tom Hood, and Gary Brown. They all tell the same story. March 21, 1966, was a terrible day for us because of the great men who gave their lives. As bad as it was for us, it was a catastrophic defeat for the North Vietnamese Regiment. We may have taken the lives of as many as 1200 men. Those soldiers, if allowed to live, would have likely placed many more names on the Vietnam Memorial Wall. I am proud to have played a part, although small, in keeping a few names off that black granite Wall.

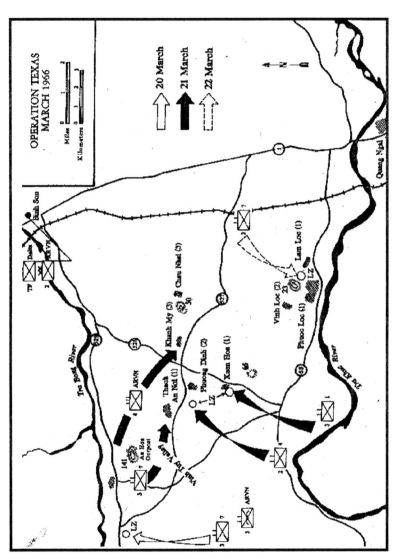

Former Commandant of the Marine Corps, General P. X. Kelley called Operation Texas three of the most intense hours of the Vietnam War. Echo Company led the assault on the Phuong Dinh village complex on March 21, 1966. After action map was prepared by Jack Shulinson, US Marines in Vietnam.

Chapter Ten
The Road Home

The trip to Chu Lai was the first helo trip I had made lying on my back. There was room for two stretchers, and I was in the right rear on the floor. I couldn't see out the door and that made me really nervous the entire flight. Those old 1950s vintage, pregnant-looking birds were big, slow targets and were always landing with more holes in them than when they took off. When I was sitting up, I knew there was little chance of an incoming round hitting me. I had on a flak jacket and sat on reinforced steel seats. Now I was sprawled out on my back and thought the odds of me taking another round were multiplied because there was more of me unprotected and exposed. We landed safely, though, without incident on the beach LZ at the air base.

I was unloaded quickly and taken into a large hot, dark olive green tent where a Navy doctor quickly started examining me. My boots were removed and the doctor started gently sticking me with a needle. He asked if I felt anything. I told him that I hadn't felt anything below my armpits since being shot about three hours earlier. "When is my feeling coming back, sir?" I asked calmly. He said he didn't know, but was sending me to the large Navy hospital in Da Nang. There I was likely to have surgery to remove the bullet which was still in me. He then started working on another Marine.

I laid on that table for another thirty minutes before being carried outside and then aboard a 47A helicopter. This was the first time I had been that close to a Chinook. It looked to be three times larger than a CH-34 and had a ramp in the rear to enter. In no time we were landing in Da Nang. In all that time I never thought I lost consciousness, and there was almost no pain. I wasn't afraid; I knew everything would be okay. I had an inner peace that words can't describe.

It was about 1700 hours when we arrived at the hospital. The helicopter was full, with maybe thirty injured Marines. Many were on stretchers, but most were seated. I was carried to the front of the hospital and met by a triage team. We were out in the open with the stretchers placed close to the building to take advantage of the shade.

When it came my turn to be examined, the triage doctor was exasperated and in a hurry. He read what was on my Chu Lai tag and then started pinching me. "Do you feel this? No. This? No. This? No. We can't get to you until sometime tomorrow. Someone will be by to talk with you later," he said. He then quickly turned to another wounded Marine. I wanted to ask how long it would be before I could return to my company, but he didn't give me a chance.

Thirty-six years later I realized why the doctor was in such a hurry. There were over two hundred casualties that day and very few operating rooms. Seventy-three of the wounded were from Echo, but I don't remember seeing any of them at Da Nang. Fred Price, the Second Platoon operator, said he was there, right next to me and remembered me asking, "When am I going to be able to get my feeling back?" but I don't remember seeing any familiar faces. Some may have been flown directly to the hospital ship floating about ten miles off the coast.

The initial doctor had to prioritize the worst injured and give more attention to those in life-threatening conditions. My spinal injury was not immediately life threatening. Only one kind of doctor could help me, and there was just one neurosurgeon at Da Nang that particular day. He had the responsibility of the head injuries as well as the spinal cord ones. In reality, they probably thought there wasn't anything anyone could do for me and there was help available for the others. I was sent to x-ray and afterward brought back outside and again placed next to the building. I don't remember them giving me anything for pain, but they must have. No later than 1900, I had passed out because I don't remember seeing the sun go down.

At 0300 I was awakened and placed on a gurney that was being rolled on a wooden floor. A bunch of corpsmen cut off my clothes and washed me up. They asked me some questions as they were preparing me for surgery, but I don't remember what. I didn't know why I was being operated on other than they were going in to remove the bullet. I just had so much peace about everything. Maybe that was why I was not more curious. I knew whatever happened, I was going to be fine. Everybody was in a hurry. There was no time for a preop conference with the anesthetist or the surgeon. They gave me a shot, and I was long gone before ever entering the operating room.

Sometime early the next morning, a corpsman awakened me and took my vital signs. I was on my stomach in a special bed called a Stryker frame. In this bed, a person could be turned over without lifting him. It was labor saving because only two people were required to operate the turn, no matter how big the patient. A frame was placed on top of the person, secured, and then flipped. There was a hole cut in the head of the bed to put my face partially through so I could breath easier. I was drowsy, but knew something was terribly wrong. All I wanted to do, however, was go back to sleep and deal with the problems later.

Thirty minutes later the same interruption. The smiling corpsman kept apologizing for waking me, but said it was something that had to be done. He called me a Geiger Tiger and wanted to know if I was ever stationed at Camp Geiger, N.C. *Why is this man talking down to me and in such a pitiful tone?* I wondered. *I have just returned from battle and deserve more respect than what he is giving me. When I feel a little better, I'll straighten this young man out,* I determined. After four or five of these interruptions, each time calling me "my big Geiger Tiger," I was almost fully awake. When I had fully expelled the drowsiness I realized he was just trying to carry on a conversation and keep me alert.

Never in my life had I felt so bad. My throat and neck hurt, my arms were on fire, and I could barely breathe lying on my belly. I told my feet to move and they wouldn't. I couldn't feel them! "Don't I need to get up and use the head?" I asked. It had been twenty hours since I had relieved myself. The knockout stuff was wearing off, and I was getting this persistent feeling that something was horribly wrong. I was suffocating on my stomach. There were some other neurosurgery patients on the ward, and I didn't want to disturb them, but I had to get over onto my back. I called the Geiger corpsman and demanded to be turned. He couldn't do anything until the doctor came in to check on me. "Go and get him," I ordered. Not long afterwards the surgeon came in and reluctantly had me turned on my back. I knew if only I could lie on my back the pain would ease up. I was wrong.

I didn't know it at the time, but my surgeon had been up all night saving Marine lives. He had to be exhausted. He was really put out with me because I was so adamant about turning over. He said I would have to learn to sleep on my stomach in order to avoid bed ulcers. *What is this man talking about? I will be out of here in no time,* I thought to myself. He said another reason for me to lie face down was to avoid pneumonia. Now that made more sense than the bedsore thing.

He pulled the sheet down and started examining me. With a needle he started pricking me and asking if I felt it. Over and over the answer was no until he got a few inches from my chin. "When will I get my feeling back, sir?" I asked.

He replied, "It's too soon to tell." He told me the bullet was really difficult to dig out. It was so badly mangled and spread out, he thought it might even be shrapnel. The incision was much larger than he wanted to make in order to remove all the metal. He had done a procedure on my neck called a lamenectomy to fuse the shattered bones back together. He explained that the path of the bullet caused it to brush against the vertebra, which is the group of bones surrounding the spinal cord. The vertebra at the thoracic one and cervical seven level in turn pushed against the spine and put it into shock. My spinal cord was not severed. He reported there was some bleeding above the fused area but thought going there would do more harm than good.

I wanted to know why I was hurting so badly. Yesterday evening I felt almost no pain. Now, my arms and the top of my right hand felt like they were burned. Just the lightest touch sent me into misery that I had never in my life experienced. It felt like the outer layer of skin was gone and there was nothing there but nerve endings. It felt worse than a toothache! Doc said that it sounded like hypersensation from the surgery and hopefully it would gradually disappear. He would order some pain medication and promised to check in on me in a few hours. He told me on his next trip back, I had to be turned. Lastly, as soon as I was able, I would be transferred to a hospital close to home.

"Would Memphis, Tennessee, be close enough?" he asked.

I said, "Yes, sir."

Five minutes later I had a shot of Demerol. In a few minutes I could rest but not enough to sleep. I reviewed what the surgeon had said. What I had didn't sound too bad. The spine being in shock didn't sound bad at all. When I asked when I would get my feeling back, he didn't say never. He did say I wouldn't be going back to Echo because I was going to Memphis. I thought maybe I could recuperate at home, after all I did have forty days leave built up.

I could see some of the other guys in the ward and they seemed to be worse off than I was. They all had head wounds, and I was sure some would not make it. I believe I was the only paraplegic on the ward. I glanced around the hospital. It looked as if it were a movie prop for a jungle hospital. The floors were plywood built up about three feet off the ground. The sides were 2x4s placed every four feet with screen wire attached to keep out the mosquitoes. The roof was corrugated tin. It all looked very temporary, but clean and efficient.

In less than a hour the Demerol wore off. The pain I was experiencing was absolutely unbearable. The longer I laid there the worse I hurt. I called the ward corpsman over and explained the shot had worn off and I needed another one, right then!

He said, "Your doctor left orders for one shot every four hours. Besides, that drug is highly addictive and you sure don't want to get hooked on something that powerful. Trust me, things will get better. Most guys experience the same things you are after surgery."

I nodded and tried to get my mind off the pain. I learned quickly to not let anything touch my arms. I also noticed it helped if I didn't move. Lying still wasn't a big problem because I could only move my arms, fingers, and head. Still I wanted to scream, but couldn't! If I had only been in a room by myself, I believed that I could have screamed the pain away. What a mess my life was turning out to be, but somehow I had confidence that everything would get better.

As the day progressed, the heat from the tin roof started to really bake us. There was no breeze coming through the screened walls. I learned first hand one side effect of being paralyzed was the inability to perspire very well. I was retaining the heat because I couldn't move and couldn't sweat. They were keeping me in fluids and washing my face often; however, I was getting uncomfortably hot.

A corpsman decided to move a large fan closer to my bed. When he turned it on, I almost passed out. The wind hurt my arms even more than touching them. It felt like thousands of needles were taking turns sticking and scraping me on open sores. This was turning out to be the worse day of my life. I couldn't move or feel 80% of my body and the other 20% was in sheer agony. I hurt so badly, but couldn't cry or release my emotions. I had IVs in both arms and a tube in my bladder to let my urine out. Someone had to feed me and bathe me. I thought, *Please don't ever let me see another day like March 22!*

I was experiencing some tough times, but not nearly as much as my parents were back in Tennessee. Mom learned to type the year I was away. Either she or Dad sent me at least five letters each week I was away. Mom said it was good practice for her typing skills. I believe it was good therapy for her, and I benefitted by keeping up with all the happenings in Morristown. They sent care packages that the whole platoon looked forward to. Pecan pies, Tang drink mix, cookies, Kool Aid, and candies by the pound were just a few items I received. Mom watched some documentary on *Marines in Vietnam* that revealed how lonely we all were supposed to be, and how not many guys received letters or packages from the home folks. My parents determined that I would always have a successful "mail call."

I noticed from Mom's letters that she was becoming very fragile. I never told her what we were really doing. I was careful to only write about the mundane happenings we were experiencing. From her correspondence I could tell that I was almost all she focused on. She watched every program about Vietnam, read all the articles about the Marines, watched the morning, noon, evening, and late news every day, and even subscribed to Leatherneck Magazine. I wondered how she would take the fact that I was injured. The more I thought about her, the more concerned I became.

The morning of March 22, 1966, Mom saw a man walk past the living room picture window. Dad had been gone to work for a few hours, and my little sister had just gotten up for the day. The man was a Marine Captain in uniform from the reserve unit in Knoxville. He rang the doorbell. The door was open but the storm door was locked. Mom started to scream and hold onto Terri. During World War II and Korea, the only visit the family received was when a death occurred. She said, "Not my Randy, no, no, no, no!"

Captain Krolak said, "Please unlock the door; he is alive, it's not as bad as you think."

Mom let him in but could not stop crying. Nothing would calm her down. The officer asked for the number of Dad's workplace and called him. He told him that I had been wounded seriously the day before, was in good hands in Da Nang, and would be coming back to the States as soon as possible. He asked Dad if he would speak to Mom. He did, but also could not calm her. Dad was one hour away and left for home immediately. No one can remember why so many neighbors and friends came to the house so quickly, but they did. With others caring for Mom, Captain Krolak left.

My sister Vicki was picked up at school. My grandparents came down with uncles and aunts. Aunt Jean, who worked at a hospital, reported that the condition "serious" wasn't bad. The label "critical" was the word one wanted to avoid. "Critical means life threatening, while serious indicates he will live," she told everyone. Surrounded by family and friends, Mom was repeatedly assured I would be all right; still she could not be consoled. She cried uncontrollably all that afternoon.

For months, really years, Mom would break down and start crying and not be able to stop. Looking back, Dad should have gotten professional help for her. The signs of a "breakdown" were there for months even before I was injured. Dad thought everything would be okay when she realized I was safe and back in the States. He was wrong. After thirty-six years, Mom still has frequent moments where she can't control her emotions. I hated that I caused her so many problems.

Sometime during that second day a priest came over to my bed. He was the first person I had seen in the last twenty-four hours that wasn't in a hurry. He pulled up a seat and started chatting. He wanted to know where I was from, how old I was, if I was looking forward to going home, and could he do anything for me.

"Would you write a letter to my Mom and Dad for me?" I asked.

He pulled a pen and tablet out and asked me to talk slowly.

I started, "Dear Mom and Dad, I was shot yesterday and am in the Navy hospital in Da Nang where I am getting good care. I will be as good as new in no time. Please do not worry. They say I will be transferred back home in a few days. The most wonderful thing happened to me yesterday. God saved my soul and now I am going to heaven. When I get home I will tell you all about it. I guess you have noticed this is not my handwriting. A priest is writing this for me, but they are my words. Love, Randy."

Late that afternoon, the neurosurgeon and three corpsmen brought the upper frame and placed it on top of me. The doctor said he was concerned that my lungs were filling up with fluid and I would be less miserable on my stomach than if I stayed on my back and developed pneumonia. They started to turn the bed and the head came unlocked and I was dropped on my face. I screamed in panic! I tried to break the fall but none of my reflex mechanisms worked.

The fall didn't harm anything because I was locked into the frame. What it did do was to let me know how helpless I had become. Some way, somehow, they fixed the frame and placed me on my belly. I lasted no more than ten minutes until I was begging to turn back over. My face was locked into the opening at the head of the frame and all I could see was the plywood floor. There was no way to lay that protected my arms from being touched. I tried to get the corpsmen to understand I could barely breathe. I had so much agony and fear that I started to panic! I knew the other injured men were hurt much worse than I was, but I was losing control.

Somehow, I held on for two hours until the group turned me back over, this time without dropping me. The sun was going down and the ward had really cooled to the point that it was almost comfortable. The Demerol should have let me rest enough that I could sleep. It just was not strong enough, because I don't remember sleeping any after waking up from surgery. I was in Da Nang for four days, and I am sure I dozed off from exhaustion, but my memory was of being awake day and night the whole time.

Nobody seemed to understand why my arms hurt so badly. That was frustrating! I knew how much I hurt and it wasn't just in my mind. I felt like the staff thought I was not being tough enough. Looking back and remembering the condition of those other guys on the ward, I can understand why my ailments were shrugged off. I think one of the Marines there lost both eyes and the top of his head in an explosion, and he may not have been the worst. Compared to the others, I was in great shape and here I was complaining and requiring too much attention. I soon learned to treat myself. As long as I didn't move my arms and kept the fan and sheet off them, I was better able to tolerate the pain.

The next few days were more of the same. Each time I was locked in the Stryker and flipped, I experienced a panic attack. I wonder why they didn't give me something to knock me out when I was turned? The two hours spent on my belly never got easier, but I did stop complaining. I don't remember why I didn't ask for something to help me sleep. At night, different corpsmen would pull up a seat when they saw that I was awake and spend a lot of quality time with me. They weren't curious at all about what the Marines in the field were going through. I don't even remember them asking me about what happened to me.

These men saw the worst part of war and probably were just as traumatized as those of us who were on the front lines. They mostly just talked about what they were going to do when they got home. One of the best corpsmen was a giant, six foot six, and weighed 350 lbs. He talked about liberty in the Philippines and had some tall tales to spin. He sometimes accompanied the injured guys to Clark A.F.B. and stayed over a few days. I had a story about the Philippines that could top any he told, but I never let on I had even visited there.

There was a cold water fountain at the entrance to the ward. Each day that I was in Da Nang there was a twelve or maybe thirteen-year-old Vietnamese boy who stood next to the fountain. He was neat and clean, and I believe he wore regular shoes, which was unusual. He filled pitchers full of cold water and made sure none of the patients were thirsty. He was awfully nice to me. With the temperatures soaring under the tin roof, cold water probably saved many patients from heat strokes. I know it made my life much more bearable. The kid asked me at least 100 times each day if I was okay, and if he could help me drink my water. I thought, *How ironic that I came over here to protect people like this child and hopefully make their lives better. Here in my last days in country, one of them is doing that for me and is definitely making my life better.*

On my last day in Da Nang, Doc Collins visited. What was left of Echo Company was transferred to an area just south of Da Nang. They were given a well-deserved, light-duty assignment of protecting a small bridge for a few days. Doc sneaked away and caught a ride to the hospital. I was glad to see him. I wanted to know what happened to my friends, those who made it and those heroes who lost their lives.

Doc was the first person I had seen that was on Operation Texas and would be the last one for nearly thirty-six years. I asked if he knew how I got hurt. He thought a machine gunner found the Lt. and me at the same time. He thought the bullet hit Lt. Brown's arm and then bounced into me. He said that the corpsman that helped me went back to the front and was shot between the eyes. Sgt. Wilson, Gunny Howard, and Lance Corporal Brown were among many friends who were killed.

I probably had just had my "shot" and misunderstood what he told me. I told Collins' version to so many people, schools, churches, and other groups and most of it was wrong. Corpsman Martin, who helped carry me to safety is alive today; however, another platoon's corpsman, Garold Hann, was killed that day.

In late spring 1966, President Johnson visited some of us wounded Marines. After his visit many newspapers wanted to know and publish my story. They got Doc's version or the one I misunderstood. No big deal, I was just glad to see a fellow brother who had put a lot of effort into coming to see me. Jerry Collins was everyone's friend and we all were proud he was our "Doc." It was April, 2002, before I learned the actual events of March 21, 1966. Brigadier General Gary Brown told what happened to Echo and me that day.

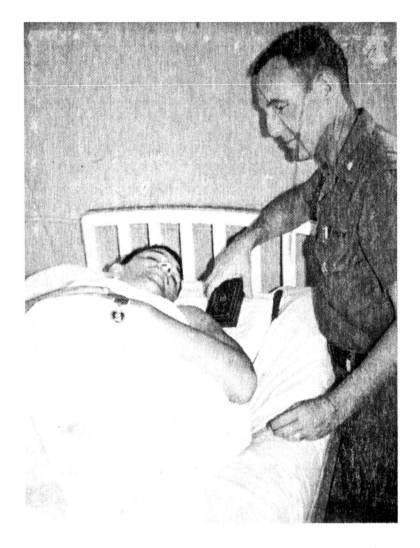

Here I am being awarded the Purple Heart by the head of the Da Nang Naval Hospital. Notice the huge white spots on my left arm. Those were week-old mosquito bite marks.

On March 26, the "giant" corpsman informed me that I was being flown out to Clark that afternoon. He was going with me as my escort and both of us were happy about that. He talked non stop on the flight over about what he had planned for liberty. I was glad to have a friend and someone who would not drop me. To be so large, this guy handled me like nitroglycerine — very carefully. We landed after dark and were met by an ambulance. The hospital at Clark AFB was one of the largest military ones in the world. I was gently placed in a real bed. There were three other Marines in the room. I don't remember how badly they were injured, but I assumed they were in bad shape, being in the neurosurgery section. I spent four days there, and I remember very little about my stay.

Clark's good points were that it was air conditioned and permanent with no plywood floors. I felt very secure in this huge complex. This place had everything that a Johns Hopkins caliber hospital had. The Air Force had so many medics there that one never had to wait for anything. The neurosurgeon sent me right off to x-ray and went through the "feel this" routine. He did tell me he understood why my arms hurt so badly, but said there wasn't anything that would help them this soon after surgery. I asked if a medic would run a large pan full of warm water and let me lay them in it. I thought that would help. The doctor said he would order that done but repeated, nothing would help me right then. He was right, unfortunately. The shots weren't helping at all. As long as I could avoid anything touching me I could stand the pain.

The only bad thing about Clark was being in a small room at night. The door was closed and the lights were turned out around 2100 hours. I still was not sleeping and not having anyone to talk to or anything to do made me concentrate on the pain. I welcomed the few times at night the medics came in and checked on me.

After a few days at Clark, I was flown to Yokosuka, Japan, and then on to Travis AFB outside of San Francisco. On the ten-hour flight to the States we were all placed on stretchers stacked five high and were strapped in tight. I dozed off for a few minutes after takeoff and was startled by a kid suffering from shell shock. He had escaped from his stretcher and the flight nurses were wrestling with him. He screamed and yelled for a little while after they locked him back in to his stretcher. They must have given him a shot of something because the rest of the trip there was little noise. While the commotion was taking place I mistakenly heard a nurse say, "We will be landing shortly and we all need to hold on tight." I "held on" for hours until I asked an attendant how long to Travis. He said, "Six more hours." That was the most miserable flight I ever made.

We landed at Travis late on the 30th of March. The next morning the plane was on the way to Denver where they unloaded some patients. I remember when they opened the plane door, those of us still inside almost froze; it was so cold and at such a high altitude. We landed and spent that night somewhere in Illinois. We left early the following day for Millington Naval Air Station outside Memphis and arrived there just before noon. That was some 12,000 mile trip!

An older Pontiac ambulance painted battleship gray pulled up along side of the plane. Two local corpsmen came aboard, lifted me onto their stretcher, and whisked me off to the small base hospital. A nice, polite, smiling older doctor met me and immediately started the "feel? feel? feel? No, no, no," routine. After x-rays, I was taken to a private room. That was just what I didn't want. I was scared, totally dependent, and in the back of my mind I had figured out how horrible paraplegia was. I wanted to be with someone who would talk with me.

The doctor came into my room and told me they were not set up to care for me in Millington. He was an orthopedic surgeon and I needed a neurosurgeon. As soon as transportation could be arranged, he would send me to the top Navy hospital around Bethesda, which was located outside of the nation's capital. It was such a great place that Presidents were treated there. He asked the corpsman standing next to me to clean me up and get me ready to see my parents who were waiting in his office.

In walked Mom and Dad and at first they didn't know what to say or do. I was in a circular bed that was scary looking. I was naked with only a sheet over me and had a drainage tube connected to a urine container that was attached to the bed. I felt very unmanly.

Big tears started to roll off Mom's cheeks and I said, "I'm okay, Mama, I really am." I reached for them and let both hug me to show them I wouldn't break. Dad's appearance was terrible. His eyes were swollen and red and his face looked as if he had slept on it. I thought it was from the twelve-hour overnight trip from Morristown.

Years later, Mom told me why he looked so bad. The Navy doctor had a conference with them while the corpsman was getting me ready. He bluntly told them that I was as good as I would ever be. He said, "Your son will never get out of bed, much less walk again." He showed them my x-rays and convinced them he knew what he was talking about. All they knew from the telegrams the Marines had sent was that I was seriously injured. Dad lost his composure and broke down. Mom said she never saw him cry that way. He thought my life was over, and if mine was, his was, too. Soon Mom joined him. After a few minutes they had their crying behind them because, according to her, the main thing was not to upset me.

With the ice broken, the welcomes and are they treating you ok, out of the way, we had a great visit. They wanted to know all about what happened on the 21st. Of course, I told them Collins' version. I was so proud to tell them that God had not only saved my life, but my soul as well. Somehow, I told them I wanted to make up for all the heartache I had caused them. I was truly ashamed of my life and the things I had done, but at the same moment I was proud and felt blessed because of the second chance I was given. I assured them that I would walk again and be as good as new. With God on my side how could I lose?

I think I did all the talking during their visit. These were great parents and they raised me to be more than I had turned out to be. I promised myself that I would try to never disappoint them again. We spent five hours together catching up on the last fifteen months. The thing that stands out most about our visit was how strong Mom was. Dad left the room a few times to pull himself together, but she never left. I thought, *I'm home now. This is the greatest country in the world and tomorrow, in Bethesda I'll find out what it is going to take to get me up and running again.*

Chapter Eleven
R&R
Recuperation and Rehabilitation

In April, 1966, Bethesda Naval Hospital was one of the best in the US military system. I felt confident and hopeful being sent there. The hospital was segregated, with the officers, members of Congress, and the President housed in a tower, and the enlisted men located in the main part of the hospital. The tower consisted of private rooms and extra-tight security. The enlisted men were stationed on long wards which had maybe forty beds. There were plenty of men to talk with on the ward and that was great for me. I would have hated a private room. I arrived in late afternoon and was immediately laid on a Stryker frame. The first evening and night was spent talking to the nurses and corpsmen about what it was like "over there."

About 0900 the next morning, I met the neurosurgeon who, I hoped, would make me whole again. He was Commander Onerfrio, a tall, wiry, clean-shaven, gold-wire-rim-glasses-wearing, thirty-five to forty-year-old doctor. He reminded me of a Harvard professor, only smarter. I was given the "feel this" routine, and then sent off to x-ray. He walked beside me and small talked along the way. Doctor Onerfrio had the technician take pictures of my neck and back from every imaginable angle. Afterward he personally wheeled me to his office. While we waited on the x-rays to be delivered, he talked to me about my surgery. He knew my doctor in Vietnam and thought he was one of the best neurosurgeons around. He stood close to me and said my loss of feeling was due to the bullet pushing the lower cervical vertebra into my spinal cord. It had caused a bruise but no cuts on the cord. That didn't sound so bad.

The x-rays arrived and Dr. Onerfrio inserted them into the x-ray light boxes. He started talking to himself saying, "I see, yes, okay, good, great job, hum, umm." This went on for an eternity. He then turned toward me and told me how fortunate I was to have had this type of treatment in a combat hospital. He said, "I believe in being honest with my patients, so here is the news. You will never walk again. You may get some return, but the odds are against you. Usually, if there is return of feeling it is in the first few days, and you have been hurt for almost two weeks."

I interrupted, and said, "Sir, I will walk again. I have a nice savings account and would like to see a doctor from Johns Hopkins. How do I arrange that?"

He said, "I know many on the neuro staff there and will accomplish that for you, but you won't get any better treatment than here at Bethesda." He went on to say, "Your life is not over. You'll be able to drive a car, work at a job, further your education, maybe father children, and a whole host of other things."

"Doctor, I will walk again," I said politely. He told me he hoped that I was right and would do everything in his power to see that I would.

He rolled me to the ward by himself. He discontinued the Demerol. I told him it wasn't strong enough anyway. He thought my arms would soon stop hurting and was surprised they were causing me that much discomfort. He thought they were sore from all the handling of my spinal cord during surgery. They were highly sensitive to touch but at least I could feel them.

I was changed from the uncomfortable Stryker to a circular electric bed which required only one person to complete a turn. He promised to get me up in a chair as soon as my wounds and neck healed. He estimated in one month I would be starting physical therapy. I liked that man and never again asked for another doctor. I was supposed to recuperate, take it easy, and build up my strength.

Nothing went according to plan. After two weeks, the large wound where the bullet was removed slowly closed. My appetite for food was weak, but coming around. That spring in Washington was constantly rainy and depressing. On a rare morning that began with sunshine, the staff said I could start PT early with some light weights. I thought, *This is the start of my recovery.* I had an urge to get up, put on my red shorts, gold Corps tee shirt and run around the hospital building a few times. That sunny morning I felt as if I could have run four miles without breaking a sweat.

That afternoon I, along with the doctors and nurses, was fighting for my life. About three in the afternoon I felt something like a dull razor blade rip open the upper part of my back. As soon as I screamed, the nurse ran and brought back Dr. Onerfrio. Blood clots were breaking off and trying to get to my lungs. Dr. O had me full of something intravenously in moments. I had day and night attention for quite a few days. My arms were now throbbing even more from all the needles and blood tests which were being taken every four hours, twenty-four hours each day. I couldn't make myself eat or drink much of anything. My strength really took a nose dive.

A few weeks later, I developed a fever that wouldn't go away. No matter what they gave me, my temperature kept rising. Finally it was in the 105-106 range. I would burn up for a while and then I'd freeze and shake uncontrollably. A large tub with ice and alcohol was brought into the ward and my whole body would be placed in the bath. An hour later, the process was repeated. I don't remember when or how, but in a few days my temp came down for good.

I noticed two things after the prolonged high temps. My memory took a nosedive. I forgot what my friends looked like and important things seemed to be erased. It also took weeks before any strength returned. I dreaded mealtime because well-meaning staff would not take "no" for an answer when I refused to eat.

My luck didn't fare any better in June. The physicians at Bethesda were top of the line. The orderly staff, however, was never around long enough to understand how to treat paraplegia. Bethesda was a teaching hospital and the student corpsmen would spend about three weeks in each profession. Just as they "got it" they were gone to Orthopedic, Plastic Surgery, or some other group. During the times I was "out of it," I rarely was turned or moved. On one Saturday morning, Dr. O was showing a guest neurosurgeon from Italy his patients, pointing out their problems and treatments. When he came to me, he noticed my feet were pressed tight against the board at the foot of the bed. He unwrapped my leggings and told the nurse he wanted to see the corpsmen who were supposed to care for me the past few days. My heels had turned black and when I was turned over, my bottom was one big sore. I never found out what happened to my caregivers, but I could not ever remember Doctor O being so angry.

I was moved to the plastic surgery ward and had skin-graft surgery on each heel. The head nurse, Lieutenant Crabtree, had me placed on my stomach and ordered me not to turn over for five weeks. They thought keeping pressure off the ulcer would allow it to heal. If that didn't work, a skin graft on my bottom would be next. I knew all of that, but to lie face down for five weeks would be impossible, or so I thought. I told her there was no way anybody could lay that way. She was unyielding and kept repeating, "If the sore doesn't heal properly, you'll have problems the rest of your life." She threatened that I'd never be able to sit up in a chair if my rear end wasn't completely well. Crabtree didn't understand that sitting in a wheelchair wasn't important to me since I was going to walk again.

The Washington D.C. area had thirty-three straight days of hot, humid temperatures over 90 degrees the summer of 1966 and that was a record. The enlisted wards were not air conditioned, and I could not tolerate a fan. Words cannot describe the misery of lying face down and being so hot. I was given some strong sleeping pills that helped me sleep, but I hated that nurse. Thirty-six years later, I have never had a skin ulcer, and I can thank Lt. Crabtree for that and for being stronger than I was.

Sometime before July 31, a Marine sergeant from Headquarters visited me. He said that I was going to be medically retired at the end of the month. I protested, "There has to be some office job I can do until I get over this. I don't want out, not just yet. Is there any way I can make Corporal while I'm recuperating here?" I wanted to be a non-commissioned officer so badly. I really wanted to wear that red stripe down the sides of my dress blue trousers. He said because I had only a short time left, rank advancement wasn't possible. He couldn't think of a position I could fill either. "Your paperwork has already been processed and no one can reverse it at this late date," I was told. What a lousy day. I was on my stomach, miserable, hot, and I was being told I wasn't good enough to remain a Marine. What a rotten tour of duty Bethesda was turning out to be. I came here to get well, not experience this kind of mess.

After the six week exile on the plastic surgery ward, I was back with Dr. Onerfrio. I now had the strength to tackle physical therapy full blast. Every day we added more to my regimen and my upper body was getting very strong. One day about a week before I left Bethesda, I was doing pushups in my bed. I pulled myself upon my knees and was holding my body up with my upper body strength. Dr. O walked over and said he had never seen someone with my level of injury do the things I was doing. He said, "At first I didn't give you a chance, but if anybody can beat this, I think you can." I heard what I wanted to hear; he said I would walk again, or did he?! My next stop would be the Memphis VA hospital. My physical therapist said Memphis specialized in spinal cord treatment and was one of the best Spinal Cord Centers in the country. They used a lot of water therapy, and he hoped I would recover everything there.

There were so many good things that happened to me at Bethesda. I had so many visitors that one would think I was a celebrity. Mom stayed a long time. Dad knew she needed to be there and I hope I helped her. There were a few times I wished she had stayed in Morristown, though. One afternoon, I dozed off for a few moments. The Marine next to me, Skip Grove, much later told me I would talk in my sleep and the language I used embarrassed even him. Mom sat through many of those expletive-laced times and never told me what I was doing. No one would wake me because I was sleeping so little. Another regret took place one morning when I unintentionally caused her to go ballistic. I decided to pull the sheet over my head in order to be by myself and think. The ward was always loud with forty patients and all the staff doing their thing. She walked over to my bed and saw the sheet pulled over my head and I was not moving. Washington, D.C. thought they were experiencing a earthquake. Dr. Anderson, the chief doctor, had to calm her down.

On Easter Sunday my grandfather, Daddy Black, visited. It was about mid-morning and I was lying face down counting the black and tan linoleum tile squares on the floor. Suddenly, I recognized the sound of his walk as he entered the ward. Daddy Black was the most confident man I've ever known and his walk was so distinctively powerful, at once, I knew it was him. He had given up the most revered day of the year at his church to be with me. I was thrilled to tell him about my battlefield conversion and the verse I had recited before I was shot. He said, "Boy, get well now," then he knelt down on one knee, placed his hand on my shoulder, and prayed that God's will be done in my life.

Dad spent a great week with me as did my uncle, Lamar. Lamar couldn't get over the nonchalant way so many guys treated their injuries. One fellow in particular, who had a quarter of the top of his head blown off, walked around with a pack of cigarettes parked in the deep crevice on top of his skull.

One weekend, Vicki and Aunt Teresa visited. After answering all their questions, Teresa said, "Randy, you don't talk right anymore. You talk like a Yankee."

I thought, *All the ribbing I took for my Southern drawl and now I'm accused of having a Northern accent!*

Uncle John and Aunt Carol were stationed at the Pentagon and were over all the time. John had just returned from Vietnam. He spoke Vietnamese and was stationed in Saigon. He said his worst experience was one three-day stretch when their air conditioner went out. I felt real sorry for him. Aunt Wanda came up on a train. Johnny Talley, his mom, sister, and brother-in-law visited. I got lots of letters and cards almost every day. I thought, *What a lucky man I am to have all these friends!*

Marge True, between a Marine whose first name was Wesley, and me. Marge worked my arms into shape.

One lady in particular was an absolute Godsend. Marge True, for some reason, visited the hospital one evening just to see if there was something she could do to help the Cause. She came over to my bedside on one of my poorer evenings. My arms were on fire, and no matter how I laid them, they burned horribly. I had lain with them out to the side and unconsciously, rarely moved them. The staff was on me to move them as much as possible to avoid atrophy.

Marge introduced herself and the church she attended. She wanted to know why I looked so unhappy and if she could do anything for me. I told her I was fine except my arms hurt and there wasn't anything that helped them. She ask if she could try something. I agreed, then she grabbed one arm and started squeezing, twisting, massaging, pulling, and rubbing it with a lot of pressure, then the other one. She worked on my arms for a good hour. She asked if she and her family could visit me on a regular basis. Almost every day for two months, Mrs. True and her three daughters spent time with me, baked cookies for the guys on the ward, and massaged my arms. The pain lightened during the massage sessions, but it always returned later. I did, however, regain my strength and movement in both arms mainly because a nice lady and her daughters cared and were willing to help.

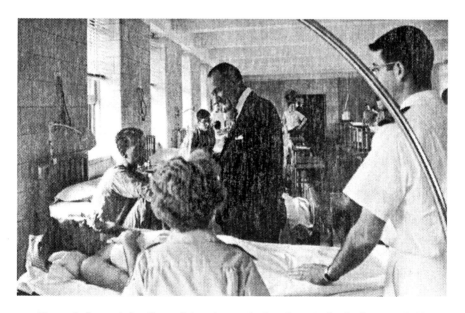

From left to right, I am lying in a circle electric bed, Corporal Skip Groove, unidentified Red Cross Nurse, President Johnson, and Dr. Onerfrio.

President Lyndon B. Johnson visited the ward one day. The man was so tall, confident, and strong. He was wearing a tailored blue suit, the darkest blue I had ever seen. He came over to my bed and said, "You're a Marine, aren't you?"

I answered, "Yes sir."

He then said, "Damn good fighting group. Listen, if there is ever anything you need, you let me know."

I thanked him and he turned to visit with the next patient. Right after he left, *I thought, I had a lot more to say to him than just yes sir.* Why didn't I tell him what I had personally witnessed? Why didn't I ask him to not let the men who died with me die in vain? Why didn't I point out to him that we were being asked to fight this war with our hands tied behind our backs? I should have asked him to please take politics out of the war and just let us win the war quickly. I had so much that I needed to say. Would anything I had to tell him have made a difference? Who knows?

Many famous people came by. Frank Sutton who played Sergeant Vincent Carter from *Gomer Pyle USMC* visited. I should have introduced myself as the goober the show got its idea from. Sonny Jergenson and Charley Taylor, the Hall of Fame Washington Redskins quarterback and wide receiver, spent a lot of time with me one day. They must have thought I was really sick because I didn't ask for an autograph. The Catholic War Veterans arranged for me to go to a Senators and Angels baseball game. After the game I met my hero, Lew Burdette, who won three games in the 1957 World Series for his previous team, the Milwaukee Braves. Both teams presented me with an autographed baseball.

I remember seeing Dr. O at the game. He gave up his Sunday because a doctor had to accompany us. He arranged for me to attend by securing an ambulance for transportation and a corpsman as an attendant. While the baseball players were talking with us, Dr. Onerfrio stayed in the background. What a great man. The Red Cross was always doing something special for us, as were so many groups. I remember we were shown *Cleopatra* with Elizabeth Taylor at the hospital before some theaters had it. Looking back, I have many special memories of that spring and summer. I really hated to leave, but I needed to get on to Memphis and get my feeling back.

Memphis started off wrong. On the flight down, the corpsmen clamped my drainage tube and I had a reflux. I was shaking all over when they placed me in the bed at the VA Hospital. The aid assigned to me knew how to fix the problem, but the mistake set me back in my rehab. Those Memphis aides were specialized in spinal cord treatment, unlike the Bethesda corpsmen. Some on my ward had twenty years experience, and that was reassuring. The hospital, however, was not at all what I expected. On the outside, it looked like a college campus spread out over 146 acres with hundred-year-old oak trees and a beautiful manicured lawn. The inside was another story. It was ancient, wooden, dark, and had old WWII era beds. All I could see were really old patients who just stared at me. The ward was long, with beds on each wall. Everybody was paralyzed. I thought, *What am I doing here?* Just like the first night in boot camp, I placed my pillow over my face and tried to cry, but no tears would come.

The first doctor to examine me was the chief of staff, Dr. Ben Moeller. It was Labor Day weekend, and he came in especially to check me into the hospital. I was one of the first Vietnam War patients at Memphis. He did the "feel this" routine and went over my medical records and x-rays. While he was reading, I asked about the water therapy and about how long it took the average patient to start walking. He looked over his glasses and said, "You will never walk again. The sooner you accept that, the better off you will be."

He had hit me hard, but I shot back, "You don't know me. I don't believe God created me to live in a wheelchair, and I will get up and walk out of here. My neurosurgeon at Bethesda said he believed I had a great chance to walk. My spinal cord was not severed."

He didn't say anything else, except that he wanted me to stay in bed for a week and then they would start rehabilitating me. One of the aides came over and said that every now and then they had a patient beat paraplegia, and he hoped I would walk out of there. I needed that reassurance.

The next three months were constant hard work. The Marines didn't have anything on my physical therapy program. Parris Island was a piece of cake compared to spinal cord rehab. Each mountain that I climbed, there was another one waiting to be scaled. Getting in and out of bed, turning, dressing, transferring in and out of a car, and walking in braces on the parallel bars by myself doesn't sound too hard, but it was akin to running a marathon with a gas mask over my face. I entered Memphis weighing about 130 pounds, and all the strenuous exercising put at least 20 pounds back on. The food was much better at Bethesda, but I was never hungry there. At the VA hospital, I was always starved and ate to stay abreast of the therapy.

The hospital was an old US Army facility erected in the early part of 1942 and was constructed to withstand bomb explosions. It was spread out and the theory was, if one part was destroyed the undestroyed part would still be useful. There were eleven miles of uneven hallways and it was almost one mile to physical therapy, up hill! We were exhausted by the time the therapist got a hold of us.

My arms hurt as much as ever, but I was learning not to give in to the pain. I was given an opportunity to have a surgeon go back in and see what was causing them to constantly burn. I believed that the Da Nang doctor left a sharp bone fragment pressing the area that controlled the arms. The thought of the risk of something going wrong during the surgery and maybe losing the use of what I had left, caused me to pass on the operation.

Memphis treated not only my body, but my entire being. One of the first things they wanted for me was my high school diploma. I secured it in early November and remembered thinking, why did I not do this in 1964? For two years I had been trying to be a high school graduate. It was anticlimactic in the sense that I felt just as dumb with a diploma as the day before without one.

We had plenty of sessions with the psychological and social staff about how to handle the world beyond the hospital walls. We were taught how to dress for comfort and safety, what kind of cars to drive, and the modifications that were needed for an accessible house. We were instructed to sit and constantly move around to avoid skin breakdowns. The objective of spinal cord rehab was to make us as self sufficient as possible.

We were encouraged to take liberty and see the outside world. On November 10, 1966, the Marines from the Memphis Reserve Depot took me to the 191st Birthday Ball where I was honored. Some nurses took me to a party at the Peabody Hotel after the Ball. Nice people were always taking me somewhere. Organizations like the VFW, the DAV, various schools, and individuals were forever taking us places and throwing parties at the hospital. Elvis didn't visit while I was there, but he did drop by the hospital sometimes when he was at Graceland. Those who remember his visits said he was the most polite young man they had ever met. He always addressed the veterans as sirs.

Only one bad thing happened to me at Memphis, but it turned out to be great seven months later. My kidneys started to produce stones and one broke loose and blocked the tube to my bladder. The urologist said he had to operate and needed my parents' permission since I was under twenty-one. I told him I was old enough to fight for my country and I didn't want my parents to know about this. He said, "You're right, and to heck with these bureaucrats."

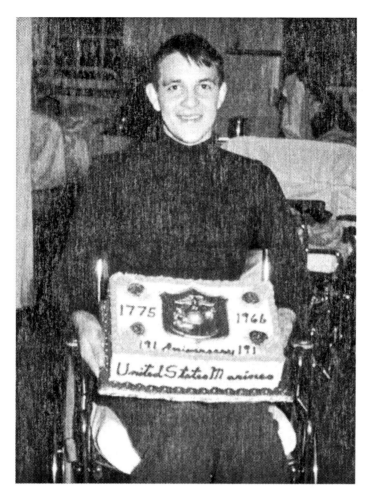

The Memphis Marines honored me with a cake on November 10, 1966.

After surgery, on the following day, Mom walked into my room. She had ridden a bus for twelve hours to see me. They had tried to call me the day I was being operated on. I hadn't called home in a while and Dad thought something might be wrong. They got in touch with an aide that everybody called Rochester, because he spoke and acted just like Jack Benny's friend. He told them I was in surgery, it looked real bad, and he didn't know when or if I would ever be back. He meant he didn't know if I was coming back to his particular ward. That sent a panic through my parents' house. So much for the right motives. I wanted to spare them from worrying; however, it had the opposite effect.

The surgery set me back a month, and I didn't leave for home until after Christmas. On December the fourth, seventeen-year-old Patty Barber came down from Dyersburg, Tennessee, to help her relatives give a Christmas party for the "boys." Her uncle and aunt were leaders in the DAV. The hospital recreation director told Patty about a young Vietnam War injured guy on ward one who couldn't attend the party because he recently had surgery. She said, "I think he would really enjoy talking with somebody his own age. Would you like to see him?" Patty agreed to meet me. We spent two hours together that Sunday evening.

This beautiful, petite, brilliant, young lady really wanted to talk with me. She thought my jokes were funny. She asked me hundreds of questions that night and was truly interested in my answers. Her diction and voice were perfect. Her posture was straight, and her eyes had that beautiful, deep, intelligent look to them. Her hair was a soft auburn red, and her smile was really sincere and gorgeous. I could not believe how much fun I was having, being with Patty. I wrote her a few days later and told her, "Meeting you was like gray skies turning bright blue all at once." What a line, but I meant it.

One of her questions was if I liked chocolate cake. Three days later I got a big tasty chocolate cake from Patty. Wait a minute, I thought, *She's beautiful, smart, and can cook!* This lady must be a angel from heaven. If that kidney stone had not become stuck, I would never have known those moments spent with Miss Barber.

My strength returned quickly, and after repassing all the strength and transfer tests, I could handle myself, and if need be, live alone. I was allowed to leave for Morristown on December 27, 1966. I got up early that morning, put on a pair of dress trousers and a blue sports coat, and said my goodbyes to the staff and patients.

The Veterans' Administration provided a ticket and an escort to Knoxville. The escort was a slim seventy-six-year-old fellow who came along to see that everything on the flight went smoothly. He was a big wrestling fan with season tickets to the Monday Nite Wrestling Extravaganza at the Memphis Coliseum. I thought at first he was pulling my leg but quickly learned he and his wife had not missed a match since 1952. He told me there were 11,000 fans at the Coliseum the previous Monday to root for their favorite wrestlers. The flight took about an hour, and after unloading, I met my family and a great family friend, Carl Osborne. Another hour and I was home among friends. After two years of serving my country and rehabbing an injury, I was home for good.

December 27, 1966, I arrived in Knoxville. From left are Dad, me, the VA escort, and Mom. After over two years of serving my country, I was home.

Chapter Twelve
What a Life!

The first month home was one hectic experience after another. Dad had remodeled our home to make it more comfortable and easier for me to get around. Anything I wanted to eat was prepared. So many people I had grown up with came by to visit. My church had a big birthday party in my honor. The local radio station repeatedly announced that, "Local Marine Randy Kington is back home." I gave my testimony the first Sunday at church. The newspaper interviewed me and had a long article about my experiences. Groups such as the American Legion honored me at their meetings. The Oldsmobile dealer came by to help me order an Olds Toronado. I was finally putting some of my gin rummy winnings to good use. Patty and I talked on the phone and corresponded. I couldn't believe how swell everyone treated me.

Everything was perfect, except that I was still in a wheelchair. I didn't want to go anywhere because I didn't want people staring and feeling sorry for me. I hated it when I noticed someone staring, and as soon as I caught them, they would turn quickly as if they weren't really looking. Many treated me like I was a freak. They were always raising their voices and talking slowly when speaking to me as if I had something wrong with my mind. Little kids would want to know why I couldn't walk. I heard "Bless your little heart" almost every time I ventured out. I got so tired of being talked down to. Total strangers asked the most intimate questions. So many referred to me as "that crippled boy." I was always polite, but over and over the same questions and stares started to get old.

I really wanted to crawl in a cave and just lick my wounds. But then again, I didn't want to be alone. I never felt sorry for myself, but I really was confused. *How long,* I kept thinking, *is it going to take for me to get well?* I knew one day it would happen, but I was running out of patience.

The rehab center in Memphis couldn't wean me from the drainage tube in my bladder, and I kept a constant bladder infection. I was sick most of that winter and spring. Family and friends pushed me to get out and do things, but I felt lousy both physically and mentally. In May, the skin grafts on my heels broke open, and I had to check back into Memphis. Dad drove with me to the hospital and parked the Toronado in the patient parking lot. He stayed with me for a day and then caught a bus back to Morristown. What a great father.

Memphis VAH was just the kind of medicine that I needed. I loved Morristown and the way most people treated me, but they didn't understand what I was going through. I needed to be around folks who understood the real problems I was experiencing.

I hated that my heels were open because it required so long in bed with them propped up to heal. Just like my kidney stone surgery though, the good things that happened during that hospitalization outweighed the bad by a ton. The first good thing was being weaned from the drainage catheter. All the times the corpsmen clamped it off and allowed my bladder to stretch also lowered my squeezing ability. I remember being clamped during the whole movie *Cleopatra* and having horrible headaches. Memphis, with its experience of treating paraplegics, would never let any of the setbacks happen that occurred in Bethesda. Shortly afterward in 1968, the Armed Services started sending all injured paraplegics directly to Veterans' Administration Spinal Cord Injury Centers. That move cut the hospital stays in half.

The greatest thing that happened on this stay was being with Patty again. After three weeks of treating my heels, I was allowed to drive off the hospital grounds for about four hours at a time. Patty and I spent every possible moment together. I remember the first evening alone with her. We went to a drive-in theater where Bob Hope was playing. I tried to impress her with the line, "Yeah, I met Bob in Vietnam and he is a real nice person." It took me a long time to work up enough nerve to kiss her. I tried the old, "let me show you how Eskimos kiss line," and it worked! She kissed like an angel.

I knew on our first date that this was the greatest woman who had ever lived. I couldn't believe my good fortune. Patty was too good to be true. She was so sweet and actually thought I was special. After only a few dates, she agreed to marry me even after I explained all the problems I was still facing. She invited me to meet her parents that weekend. That was Wednesday, and she would meet me in Dyersburg on Saturday. I called Patty's house on the next day. She was really upset. Her mom refused to meet me and didn't want Patty to ever see me again. She wanted more for her daughter than some old veteran who was also disabled. Looking back, I would want more for my child, too.

We decided to elope. I drove the eighty miles to Dyersburg and found Patty waiting. I asked if she were sure she wanted to do this, and she said, "Yes, I am and we need to be in a hurry before Daddy comes home." She left a note explaining what we were doing. I drove back to Memphis where we got our blood tests. It was getting late, so I put Patty up at a Holiday Inn and went back to the hospital and spent the night. The next morning we headed to Mississippi to get married.

I wasn't apprehensive until Patty told me that her dad carried a shotgun in his truck and he probably was out looking for us. Every brown pickup I saw, I knew it was him. I didn't want my future wife to think I was a coward, but I couldn't keep from constantly looking in the rearview mirror.

Our first stop at a Mississippi courthouse was funny. The judge told Patty he couldn't marry us because she had to be twenty-one. Patty said, "Your Honor, I have to get married," meaning her dad was going to shoot both of us if she went back unmarried. The judge thought she meant something else and said, "Little lady, your folks will understand."

We drove on to Florence, Alabama, where we found out I wasn't old enough but Patty was. The solution was to get a parent's notarized permission for me to get married. Morristown was 350 miles away, so we improvised. We stopped at a house with a sign in the front yard that read "Notary Public $5." A black gentleman answered the door. We explained our problem and he agreed to pose as my father and signed the permission papers for five dollars. We were married on June 24, 1967, with the sheriff as my witness and his clerk as Patty's. We drove back to Memphis that day and spent the night together as husband and wife.

We called her folks and agreed to have lunch at the Barbers' that Sunday. I was more nervous than a long-tailed cat in a room full of rocking chairs. What were they going to say or do to me? We pulled up in front of their house and everybody ran out to meet us. I was treated fifty times better than

I deserved. There must have been twenty-five relatives there to see Almus and Louise's new son-in-law.

I found out so much about Patty during that get-together. Running away with me was the first time she had ever disobeyed her parents. They proudly told of never having to even spank her as she was growing up. Now that impressed me because I probably averaged one per week. She graduated among the top in her class and that was in spite of taking the hardest courses such as trig, biochemistry, and advanced English. She was a beauty contest winner. Her mom let me know she had many steady boyfriends over the last couple of years.

Almus quickly warmed up to me, but Louise was grudgingly polite. Her mother got hateful with me during lunch. She had prepared an awesome meal that filled up two large tables. The only thing I wanted to eat was roast beef and mashed potatoes. I kept politely refusing the offered dishes as they were passed around, such as fried green tomatoes, cornmeal-battered fried okra, and green beans cooked with fatback. Louise stood up and looked right through me and said, "If I can go to the trouble of fixing this meal, you can go to the trouble to eat it." She, of course, was right. I tried some of those Southern dishes and went back for seconds. I think after the second or third plate of okra, Patty's mom started to warm up a bit toward me.

Her dad told us he would build a ramp into the house and that we were welcome to stay there as long as we wanted. They asked us to visit often and he would make sure the next time their house would be wheelchair accessible. He told me he was easy to get along with if I would be good to his daughter. He also said that they didn't believe in divorce.

Louise, however, was still not convinced about Patty's choice of a mate. She wanted to know how I would support her daughter. I told her I was retired from the Marines with a nice pension for life. As soon as we got back to Morristown, we were going to build a house that the VA would help us finance. I promised to be good to Patty and provide her with everything she needed. I thanked her parents for doing a great job of raising my wife. When I left Dyersburg that afternoon I felt like her folks had accepted me, and I knew I liked them.

I was so proud to introduce my five-foot-tall angel to the good people in Morristown. She fit right in. The church fell for Patty. She became active in all the groups and choir. The ladies gave her the largest household shower that anyone could ever remember. A young couple, Herman and Shirley Huskey, who had recently retired from the Air Force, took us under their

Patty, who is second from the left, at the 1966 Miss Dyersburg Beauty Pageant.

wings. We played cards 2 or 3 nights each week while feasting on Shirley's cherry pies. Their friendship was a giant building block in our lives. Their son Gary, at age 12, could beat me in gin rummy 50% of the time. So much for my foolproof card playing system.

February 1968, we moved into our new home. I had already chosen the house plan, but Patty picked out all the things that made it a home. She worked with the builder more than I did. He thought Patty was an engineering student with all the technical questions she asked. In addition to all of her other qualities, Patty had exquisite taste, something that I lacked. Visitors marveled at our ability to afford a professional decorator when, in fact, eighteen-year-old Patty chose everything.

The summer of 1967, a Morristown kid was paralyzed in a silo accident. He was sent to Boston and Dr. Ed Spatz operated on him. One year later the young man walked without any help. I asked Patty if she would go to Boston with me to see this doctor who seemed to work miracles. Being injured in the military entitled me to check into a VA hospital without all the usual red tape. I planned to stay at the West Roxbury VAH until Doctor Spatz cured me. We purchased tickets to Boston without calling ahead because I was afraid I would be put off for a few months if I asked. I figured it would be easier to ask for forgiveness than for permission. I planned to barge in and insist that I be treated immediately. I had spent over two years in a wheelchair and that was long enough. I had been hurt fighting for my country, and the least this doctor could do would be to treat me as soon as possible. I had the following few weeks all rationalized out.

We landed at Logan Airport and were in the hospital Chief of Staff's office within a fast taxi ride. The head doctor said, "You have come a long way for nothing. I know Dr. Spatz personally and it takes months to get in to see him. And you can't stay here at the hospital without something medically wrong." I told him I knew my rights and I wasn't going home until I saw Dr. Spatz. I took off a sock and showed him one of my skin-grafted heels and said, "I am 100% service connected and I believe you have to treat me, sir."

The Chief left the room and returned in a few minutes. He had called Memphis and talked to my doctor there. He must have been told that I wasn't crazy, or a trouble maker, but was determined to walk. He made a second call to Dr Spatz's office and secured an appointment for me in two hours. He said I could stay at the hospital that night and they would find Patty a room at the nurses' quarters.

We arrived at Dr. Spatz's office early. Both of us were nervous but confident. We had gone to a lot of trouble and spent money we really didn't have for this not to work. Dr. Spatz talked with us and said he was proud of his Morristown patient and his recovery. He was impressed that we had come so far to see him. He ask me a few medical questions, the entry and exit wound locations, and did a "feel this" type exam. He pulled up a chair and in a fatherly tone told me, "You realize you are a miracle, don't you? You should not have the use of your hands. No doctor can help you now, but if I were you I would be pleased that I was given so much back. I see patients every day who can't move anything, and that should have been you."

I told him that I was grateful for my arms and hands, but I had hoped he could help me walk. He asked if there was anything else he could help with. I asked, "Why do my arms still hurt?"

He said he had run across that in a few of his patients. He really didn't know why some experienced that type of hypersensitivity, but it was at the injury line in the cord and just maybe it was the nerves trying to regenerate. We both thanked him for taking the time to see us and left. That man was so nice; I knew if there was any hope, he would have worked day and night to heal me.

The words, "You are a miracle," and "You should not be able to use your hands," kept repeating themselves in my mind for the next days, months, and years. I didn't want to give up. I was no quitter, but I knew after the visit with Dr. Spatz, it probably wasn't meant for me to be whole again. I still prayed every day for years for God to heal me. I knew that for some reason, I had been given way beyond what I deserved, and most likely I wasn't a candidate for anything else. After all, God had performed more miracles in my life than most cities receive. He had saved my soul, had saved my life twice (the helicopter crash and on 3-21-66). He returned the use of my hands to me, and He gave me an angel to be my wife. He sent so many people my way who genuinely cared about and supported me. I never had the adjustment problems and bad dreams that so many of my Vietnam War brothers had. He gave me the ability to be happy and content with my station in life. I almost felt guilty when I asked for more.

The summer after meeting Dr. Spatz was a time of deep soul searching. If I were going to be a lifetime paraplegic, I needed to do something with my life that would make a difference. My options were limited to something using my mind, which was a wasted asset at that moment. My pension was almost enough to comfortably support the two of us forever. Our marriage was as sound as any I knew, but I thought, if I wanted it to grow and get even stronger, I needed to do more than just sit around and draw a check every month. I wanted Patty to respect me as much as I did her. Even after thirty-six years of nearly perfect marriage, I am still insecure. She has tons of class, is smart, talented, loving, and pretty. Her personality requires everyone to love Patty. I keep asking myself, why does she love me? Even if I had my full health, I wouldn't be good enough for her. I had to do something that would make me be more of the man she deserved. I should be working and supporting my family.

I needed to go to school to make something of myself. It had been over four years since high school, and I wasn't sure if I was intelligent enough to succeed. Patty pitched right in and agreed she would go with me and be my tutor. Before we were married, she intended to be a registered nurse with a BS in nursing. I always thought she would eventually make a fine medical doctor. She gave up those dreams in order to attend school with me. We chose a small school thirteen miles from our house, Carson Newman College, where we both majored in accounting.

College was easier than I thought. I had everything going for me. So many people wanted to make sure I succeeded. The admissions dean even volunteered to be my advisor. The college had lots of steps and barriers, but a Marine named David Sandifer met me each morning and saw to it that I was carried up them. David taught me a life-long lesson on how to accept help. I kept trying to repay him until one day he said "Stop, you'll never know how much pleasure I receive from helping you. Please don't lessen my joy by trying to pay me back." I didn't really understand what he was talking about until I found myself in a position of giving. Now when people buy my lunch or do something for me, I don't insult them by trying to even the score. Folks are forever helping me put my chair in the backseat of my car when it is so much easier to do it myself, but I understand they just want to help.

Eventually the school built ramps to my classes. I had only the responsibility to attend class, read the lesson, and do the homework. All I had on my hands before starting school was free time. I actually enjoyed the challenge and meeting so many nice people. Patty, on the other hand, attended the same classes, took all of our in-class notes, read the lessons and did the homework, corrected and typed my papers, cooked our meals, washed and ironed our clothes, kept the house spotless, and never complained. We both graduated with honors on May 7, 1972. Patty was awarded honors because she was a hard worker and very smart. I, on the other hand, owe my awards to Patty.

I had decided between our sophomore and junior year, that I wanted to teach accounting. We had taken all the basics and decided to try an accounting course the summer before our junior year. I really liked the course and determined the field of accounting would be better to handle from a wheelchair than another area of study. I wanted to teach on the college level. In order to teach college accounting, I had to get a master's degree. The University of Alabama had a great program. We applied and were accepted in the spring of 1972.

Graduate school was five times tougher and required much more time and effort to pass. Just one semester course required four thirty-page research papers. Patty was doing all of her school work, all the household chores, and correcting my papers and typing them. It was too much. After the second semester, Patty told me her heart wasn't in being a teacher or an accountant. She wanted to be a mother and raise our future children. She said it was more important for me to get a graduate degree because I had to have one to teach. If she wasn't going to school she would have more time to help me and make sure I would graduate. What she did was sacrifice her own academic achievement in order that I could attain mine. I (really we) graduated on time with an MA in accounting the summer of 1973.

Before graduation from Alabama, Carson Newman offered me a position in their business department teaching accounting and taxation. I had to give up twenty percent of my retirement income to accept the offer, but that didn't matter. My department head was Jim Coppock, and he made sure I had available all the tools that I needed to be a good teacher. He was a great boss. I taught alongside Joe Mack High, a Marine from WWII and Korea. He was my inspiration to be a teacher. I had taken five accounting courses under Mr. High and decided early that I wanted to teach and conduct myself like him. Teaching at Carson Newman was a dream come true. In 1974, I passed the CPA exam and became a Certified Public Accountant and received tenure in 1978. I was out front receiving all kinds of accolades and honors, while Patty was always in the background. Every time I received an applause, Patty was clapping the loudest.

We adopted two wonderful boys Johnny in 1974 and Josh in 1978. In addition to all her other attributes, Patty knew all about being a great mother. She did all the necessary things that encouraged both to grow up and become young men. We both enjoyed growing up again through our sons. All the school functions, tee ball, little league, pee wee football, and high school baseball, football, track, and basketball games were more fun for Patty and me than I could ever communicate. Patty and I had a great life before the boys, but with them, our lives seemed more complete.

Summer of 1978 was a turning point in my growth as a Christian. I had been saved for twelve years; however, I seemed to be stuck in neutral. I was going to church regularly, teaching an adult Bible class, serving on various committees, but I seemed to be missing the peace and joy that others were experiencing. Down deep I knew what was wrong. I was afraid of being baptized. I would have to be carried up to the small two person church baptistery and lowered into the water. I thought, *What if I'm dropped and suck water into my nose and lungs?* I had rationalized for a long time that baptism was symbolic. I was already saved, and God surely understood my fears; however, still I felt like something vital was missing and I was disobedient.

Our pastor of ten years, Reverend Jewell Travis, had accepted another ministry position and was preparing to leave Morristown. I met with him and asked him if he would baptize me before he left. He said, "We'll baptize you in Charlie Hodge's swimming pool." Why didn't I think of that?

The next day, Rev. Travis and his two sons, David and Lynn, pulled up in the driveway in a new silver and red Chevrolet Caprice the church had given him as a going-away gift. I insisted that we take my car, but he wouldn't hear of it. He said they would see to it that I was dry before lifting me back into their car.

The four of us got into the pool. The pastor said the appropriate words and gently pushed me under the water and then lifted me up. I went under knowing something was missing, but when I came back up, I felt completely full. All of those years of fear and dread when the solution was so easy. The guys lifted me out of the pool and placed me on a towel in the front seat. When we pulled into my driveway, it seemed as if I had dripped five gallons of water in their new Chevy. It probably took weeks for the carpet to fully dry. Rev. Travis never let on that he was anything but happy for me. He has had a huge part in my spiritual growth. Because I know the kind of man he is, he felt a wet seat and floorboard were a just price for my peace.

In 1980, I accepted an offer to become the tax partner at Hiram Jones and Associates, Certified Public Accountants. I was transformed from an academic accountant into a real one, and believe me, it was no easy matter. Mr. Jones showed great patience in helping me leave the ivory tower of college accounting and work in the real world.

Six years later, Patty and I opened our own practice. Both boys were in school and Patty thought she needed a challenge. She had been out of accounting for thirteen years, but no one noticed. She managed the office and ran the information systems flawlessly. I was up front with the clients, consulting, planning, and directing our programs. Patty was in the background, working twice as hard and putting in many more hours than I did. Again, I got most of the credit for the firm's success while Patty was ten times more responsible. We did have some clients who begged me to let them hire Patty for a large amount of money, but we wouldn't agree. My reason was selfish and Patty's was loyalty.

I was in a serious car crash in the fall of 1991. It took six months for me to get my vision back. When I returned to work, the drive I once had to succeed was missing. The two CPAs working for us offered to purchase the firm. We accepted the offer and retired, May 1992.

After the boys graduated and moved out of the house, we decided to sell our farm. We purchased two condos, one in Morristown and the other one in Naples, Florida. East Tennessee winters can be brutal. Now, October thru April we spend in sunny Southwest Florida. What a life!

There is a group of retired Marines who have lunch together every Wednesday, and I miss very few of the get-togethers. They celebrate the Marine Corps' birthday each November 10, dressing up, wearing ribbons and medals. When a wonderful Chosin Reservoir Marine learned I would attend the Ball wearing an ordinary blue suit, he and his wife purchased a red dress jacket for me. Joe and Deloris Buckles wanted me to be in "uniform." Joe also bought ribbons for me to wear. That was such a nice thing for them to do. Before meeting these Naples Marines, I was always proud to be a Marine but never got involved with any veterans' groups. I never thought about medals or ribbons or even what happened on 3-21-66. At the 2001 Marine Corps Ball, I found out where Gary Brown lived. We got together for the first time in thirty-six years on April 6, 2002, and after two hours of non stop sharing of memories, I decided to put my story to pen and paper.

During the summer at Bethesda, a staff corpsman told me to avoid a new student corpsman by the name of Franks. He said that the new guy had spoken up during a teaching session about the subject of keeping paraplegics alive. Franks said, "We are not doing these Marines any favors by extending their lives. Look at what they are facing; years of constant hospitalization, pain, and indignities. Think about how much they are going to cost the taxpayers. What is wrong with just letting them humanely die?"

The staff corpsman spoke up and said, "I joined the medical field to heal, not to kill!"

I've thought of Corpsman Franks often over the years. I've never shared this story with anyone. I am thankful his view was singular and I was not allowed to die. I would hate to have missed all of the lives that have touched mine, like my family, my Marine brothers, former students, clients and associates, friends, fellow church members, Johnny and Josh and their families, Gentry and Joshua my grandchildren, and most of all, Patty.

One of my favorite movies is *It's A Wonderful Life* starring Jimmy Stewart as George Bailey. His Uncle Billy lost $8,000 of the Bailey Savings and

April 6, 2002, General Brown and me together in Ellington, Florida for the first time in 36 years.

Loan's money. George was responsible and was headed to prison. He wanted to end his life until an angel named Clarence showed him what the world would have been like without him. George found out the world was a better place because of all the lives he had touched. The movie ends with his many friends making donations to a fund to save him from jail.

The last 37 years of my life has been like the end of *It's A Wonderful Life*. People have been lined up outside of my life since March 21, 1966, to give whatever it took to make me a better person. I am not so sure the world is better because of any contributions I may have made; however, I am better because of all the lives that have touched mine.

Chapter Thirteen
After *What a Life*

The editors at PublishAmerica recently gave me permission to add another chapter to *What a Life*. I am appreciative because everywhere we go, Patty and I are asked, "When are you going to write another book?" I am not sure that there is enough energy left to tackle another complete book, however, another chapter or two may come forth. It took a good year of grueling work, lots of time, and plenty of tears to finish those first twelve chapters. I'm almost 59 and have been hurt for over 39 years. I certainly agree with the person that said, "If I had known I was going to live this long, I would have taken better care of myself."

The book hit the stores on November 29, 2003. The publisher sent out a note that stated *What a Life* was in thirteen countries and all the large bookstores (Barnes and Noble, Borders, Amazon, etc.). Since November 23, 2003, Patty and I have shared our story (Life's Testimony) with numerous groups including over 80 churches, colleges, and countless civic groups. Large, small, Catholic, Episcopal, Church of God, Presbyterian, Baptist, Methodist, Community Churches, Rotaries, Kiwanis, Lions, each place seems to receive our message well. Few groups have failed to give us a standing ovation. That sounds kind of like bragging, but I believe the applause is more for the message than for Patty and me. I believe one huge reason we are made to feel so accepted is the increased level of patriotism this country is experiencing after those hijacked planes tore into the Twin Towers. It is about time!

After speaking, I generally sign copies of *What a Life*. While I am writing something personal in their book, many will share a story of their own, or about a friend's, or a family member's experience in Vietnam. Their heartbreaking accounts are repeated over and over. The betrayal and ingratitude that greeted so many of our men and women in uniform as they returned home remains difficult to forget. Spending thirteen months fighting for the greatest country in the history of mankind, and then being treated so badly, is still adversely affecting many Vietnam Veterans. In this chapter, I hope to share some of their stories in addition to what has gone on in our lives these past two years.

A few weeks before the official distribution date of November, 29, 2003, many of our friends began hearing about the project that had taken away a good year of Patty's and my life. They wanted a copy as soon as possible. Many ordered five or ten books to pass around to friends and relatives. Friends Shannon and Janice Greene, ordered 250 copies!

I asked Shannon, " What are you going to do with 250 books?"

He replied, " I'm going to send them out as Christmas presents to all of our friends and customers."

Neighbor and friend Adren Greene purchased fifty copies to give away. After almost two years, I still get great calls and comments as a result of all of those gifts. Patty and I have been truly blessed to count so many people as friends.

I received an advance delivery of 100 books the last of October, 2003. They lasted only through the first two book signings. Bob and Carol Brewer hosted the first signing for us at The Falling Waters in Naples, Florida. The 2003 Marine Corps Ball in Naples was just like a signing. So many kept coming over to our table to get their books signed. That night was a very special one. I was given the honor of introducing the guest speaker, a man that not only saved my life in Vietnam, but has become a close and dear friend. General Gary Brown shared his recollections of Operation Texas, detailing how the two of us were injured.

He began his talk by stating, "This is the first time I have ever shared what happened on March 21, 1966, with any group. There is only one person for whom I would do this—my former radio operator, Randy Kington. I believe I would do anything for him." I felt very honored and proud. The Naples Marines had asked me to contact the General and invite him to talk about our time together in Vietnam for the November 10th event. I did not realize how badly he felt about the happenings on 3-21-66, until he began sharing the story of Third Platoon, Echo Company, 2nd Battalion, 4th Marines. We lost so many great Marines that day and as their leader, then Lt. Brown felt that he could have done more. Those of us who were there know, the only way more could have been done would be if Gary Brown had been cloned.

I believe after speaking, Gary enjoyed his first Marine Corps Ball since retirement. He wore a tailor made tuxedo with his numerous medals, including two Silver Stars (nation's third highest honor) over the left breast. When the General first entered the Ballroom, I introduced him to different friends as General Brown. After a few puzzled looks like *I know this man from somewhere,* I began addressing him as "General Brown; Lt Brown in the book." Almost everyone there wanted him to sign their copy of *What a Life.*

We came back to Morristown the weekend before Thanksgiving. The following four weeks, I was given the privilege of speaking in six area churches and four civic groups. Pastor Chris Reneau invited me to speak at The Morristown Church of God (my mother's church and the church I grew up attending) and share the testimony of *What a Life.* The church was packed. The message took about thirty minutes and the congregation could not have been more attentive and responsive. For some unexplained reason, I was not at all nervous. I really felt like letting others know what happened to me was something I needed to do. I felt confirmed. Mom cried through most of the service, however, I don't ever remember her being more proud. Afterward, I began to hear the stories of others. "I was there," or "My husband, brother, or dad died from Agent Orange." "My son left a well adjusted young man. Now, he cannot get past what happened." Vietnam happened so long ago and the prevailing thought down through the years has been, *let's not think about that tragic time and it may just fade away.* I wasn't prepared for the response that morning. There were many tears shed. Four hundred people must have shaken my hand and said "Thank you for sharing your life with us." It was as if they were saying *thank you for not allowing us to forget.*

The following Sunday, Doctor Richard Emmert invited me to speak at Manley Baptist Church, our home church. Again, I was not nervous, but for some unexplained reason, I could not fall asleep the night before the service. I must have been on a high dose of adrenaline because I was not at all tired. I spoke for 30-35 minutes at each of the three services. Their reaction was the same as the previous week—awesome. I think they were most responsive to the part where I talked about Patty's lifelong sacrifice and dedication to making me into the man that I needed to be. They recognized Patty's 36 years of sacrifice by giving her a tremendous standing ovation. Patty's tears would not stop running. I believe it touched her to know that not only I knew how selfless she is, but others also. For all of us who know her, Patty is truly one of America's greatest heroes.

The stories we heard after each of the next services were heartbreaking. One Vietnam veteran told about landing in San Francisco and literally having to change into civilian clothes in order to make it through the airport. The protesters were screaming and throwing stuff at anyone who was in or associated with the armed forces. It is hard to believe there was a time in our country's history when the *uniform* was not respected. At the annual 2005, 2nd Battalion, 4th Marine Regiment Reunion in San Diego, one of the men told of two young PFCs on his flight. They were headed to Camp Pendleton, but were early and could not sign in for two days. This was their first trip to California. They asked the man seated next to them if he could recommend an inexpensive motel close to Pendleton. Within minutes, nineteen people offered these two Marines spare bedrooms in their homes. An official with the Hilton Hotel corporation was told about their plight by one of the stewardesses. He paid for luxury accommodations at a nearby Hilton and also a rental car for the two men in uniform. Thirty-five years ago, that absolutely would not have happened.

At each of the next four churches and four civic groups, the reception was fantastic. So many of my former students, friends that grew up with me, neighbors, accounting clients, business associates, fellow church and Sunday School members were in attendance. Many would remark, "I've known you for all these years and I never knew that about you, or even how you were hurt." In one of my messages I told about dealing with Vietnam and what happened to me personally. I locked away that part of my life and rarely talked or even thought about it for 36 years. If someone asked, I never made a big deal about not wanting to talk about that time of my life, but the reply was short and uncomfortable. I always assumed that I was the only one who handled adversity that way—*out of sight out of mind.*

In almost every place we visited, we heard about a relative, a friend, or even former husbands that came home from the war and also locked away that part of their life. We heard so often, "If my brother would only talk with us, or if we knew more about what happened, we might be able to do something to help." At one church a son shared how angry he was at his father. He said, "My dad has never ever talked with anyone about where he was and what he did in Vietnam, not even me his own son!" I asked what branch of service his dad was in and learned he was a Navy Corpsman. I told the son "Your dad saw the worst of war. The Marines are the first to fight and generally see the carnage they inflict on the enemy. The Corpsmen see the bloody gore, missing limbs, faces, and lives of their own men. They are the ones who zip up the body bags. No one, especially a twenty-year-old who probably had less than four months of medical training, knows how to handle that type of horror. Please be more understanding and see if your father will visit with a Veterans Administration counselor."

The past two years, we have met countless ex-wives that reported their Vietnam Vet husband just "turned in" and would not share anything about their life with anyone. It was like they were carrying a dark secret. Many of the women still have deep feelings for their former husbands. One who had remarried and had her new husband at her side, purchased a copy of *What a Life* and lovingly said "I'm going to give this to Paul and I hope it helps him."

We returned to Naples after Christmas. Speaking engagements at first were hard to arrange. We have only been Florida residents since 1998 and each year spend six months in East Tennessee. Not many Floridians know me or have heard my testimony. My grandfather was always cautious about who he invited to speak in his church. Florida pastors are equally cautious. Our Florida home church, Marco Island First Baptist Church and one of the largest Baptist churches in Southwest Florida, First Baptist Church of Naples, allowed us to share our testimony. Jeff Fletcher, a pastor at East Naples Baptist Church invited us to speak in his church and to an area pastors' conference of which he was that year's president. After the conference, we had many opportunities to speak, thanks to Jeff.

Homer Helter who owns one of the most interesting military memorabilia stores in Naples, organized a book signing for some military authors and invited me to join them. I signed books next to Korean War hero, Joe Owen who wrote *Colder than Hell*. Joe spoke non stop for four hours about his time at the Chosin Reservoir, a battle in which one Marine division defeated twelve Chinese divisions in the last months of 1950. We both dispensed plenty of books, however, if none were sold, the time spent with Joe would have been worth it. A good friend and fellow Tuesday morning coffee drinker, Carmen Fino also had a signing for me at a popular coffee shop on 5th Avenue.

Again, at each gathering, the stories about Vietnam flowed. Each time I speak, I try to let the listeners know about the plight of those Vietnam Veterans who are still hurting. After the war, an inordinate number of vets began dying from different types of soft cell cancers. After much investigation, the numbers pointed toward a defoliant Dow Chemical sold to the military called Agent Orange. The idea of destroying the hiding places of the Viet Cong was a good one—the after war results of that action, however, have been disastrous. Dow, of course claimed their research did not indicate the poison spray was unsafe to inhale and be around. The government relied on the civilian company's research and for years denied the excessive number of vets' illnesses had anything to do with their time in service. Finally, the numbers became overwhelming and the Veterans Administration began recognizing the root cause of so much sickness was exposure to Agent Orange.

If only the Government had gotten outside the Beltway and talked with the veterans and their families. Over 177,000 Vietnam Veterans according to the V A have or soon will have type two diabetes because of their exposure to Agent Orange. One veteran told me his unit spent days sleeping, eating, walking, and breathing in an area that had been cleared by spraying Agent Orange. "The place looked like a moonscape—no living organisms," He reported. If it would do that to the plants and trees, why not human lungs?

One of the most common comments we hear deals with sickness and death from Agent Orange. It seems like everyone has a relative or knows someone who has died a slow and painful death from that horrible poison. Sadly, many vets don't know what to do when they get sick. We have helped many by recommending Vietnam Vets have a toxin screen at a nearby V A Hospital. There are many types of maladies that the VA automatically assumes are the result of Agent Orange, if the vet was in country between 1965 and 1971. For example, any Vietnam Vet who is diagnosed with prostate cancer is automatically eligible for treatment at the VA. Prostate cancer is considered one of the 23 types of cancer caused by that venomous spray.

During our time in Naples, we had two reunions with old Marine friends. In January, a group spent four days with us in sunny Southwest Florida. Wouldn't you know, those days were the coldest ones of the year. General Brown, Ed Brummett (Platoon Sgt.), Ted Gray and wife Madelin, John Hollars, Ray Wyatt, and Ed Martin (Platoon Corpsman) fished, swam, ate out, visited with area Marines, and caught up on old memories. The Grays brought loads of cajun food and Ed Brummett passed around elk meat from Oklahoma. This was the first time for all of us to be with Doc Martin since the battle. At first, Martin did not remember anything about Operation Texas. Actually he said he was not there. Gary reminded him that he had rushed up to him when he was first shot. "Doc, you told me '*Lt., wrap your belt tightly around your arm and stop the bleeding. Sorry I can't stay with you; there are so many others hurt worse than you out there.* 'Remember that episode?" asked Gary. Ed recalled that moment, but little else. After the battle, Ed was transferred to the hospital in Da Nang and saw the very worst of the war's injuries. Forgetting has probably allowed Doc to sleep a little easier.

Tom, a fellow Marine, visited in April all the way from Alaska. He found Gary Brown's and my name on the internet. He decided to ride his motorcycle down; it took eleven days to finally roll into Naples. Gary came down for the first day—both of us were so honored that Tom would come that far just to visit us. Much of our time that day was spent in front of the television. Tom lives on Wrangel Island and does not own a set. The Iraqi War was in full swing and the three of us discussed our time together in Vietnam while watching the Marines fight their way toward Baghdad. Gary and I could not get over how clear Tom's memory was. He even remembered the markings on the A-4 Skyhawks that dropped napalm in front of us on March 21, 1966. Tom was the last person to see me walk. Said he would never forget the moment that I was blown off the rice paddy dike. After four days, Tom rode off toward his parents' home in Northwest Florida.

The General invited us up to meet his family on March 21, 2003, thirty-eight years after "The Battle". Gary's beautiful wife, Judy, daughter Lauren and her husband Roy, and the apple of granddad's eye, Ariel were there. What a beautiful, loving family. Many don't realize the sacrifice families of servicemen make. Constant separation, frequent moving about the world, knowing their loved one maybe in harm's way is a stress many have trouble coping with. For 32 years, not only Gary served his country, but his family as well. The Browns' bond of strength and love for each other is a testament to the entire family's dedication to the service of their country.

Before eating, all of us honored the memories of Gunnery Sergeant Howard, Sergeant Wilson, and the other heroes that gave all they had on that fateful day. John Bradley, one of the flag raisers on Iwo Jima, was once asked how it felt to be a hero. He replied, "The real heroes are the men that gave their lives for this country." The Brown and Kington families concur with that special WWII Corpsman. Gary and I agreed, every year, we would get together and honor those friends who gave their lives in the Vinh Tuy valley.

We returned to Morristown the last of May. Our first engagement was at the First Baptist Church of Morristown on the Sunday before Memorial Day. I changed my message for that special day. The sermon was titled *Please*

Do Not Forget. I began by remembering a twenty-year-old Corpsman who died on March 21, 1966, by the name of Gary Hann. There were three main points, members of the armed forces, their families, and God. I challenged all to never forget all the sacrifices these three have made down through the years. Those sacrifices are the very reason America is free today. After the service, World War II Navy Veteran, businessman, philanthropist, and friend, John Wallace invited us to eat lunch with his family. After lunch, John said, "You touched me today. Wallace Hardware does not recognize Memorial Day as one of its employer paid holidays. Starting next year, the fourth Monday of May will be a paid holiday for all of our employees."

The summer and early fall of 2004 were some of the best months of my life. Among the groups where I was invited to speak were 27 churches, 2 colleges, 12 civic clubs and a group of Paralyzed Veterans in Johnson City, Tennessee. At First Baptist Church of Sevierville, there were approximately 1600 people in attendance. The church and one of its members purchased 60 copies of *What a Life* to give to Vietnam Veterans in attendance. In September, we were allowed to speak in the church my parents attended when I was born, Mt. Olive Ministries in Cleveland, Tennessee. It had been almost 45 years since I last was in that church. In 1959, the parking lot was a graveled one, the church building's exterior was concrete block, and rarely would over 100 people attend services. Now, there is a huge auditorium, family life center with a large gymnasium, and sizeable children's church. Mom, Vicki, and her husband Denver drove down. Many people still remembered our family attending church there.

Later in September, a friend of John Hollars and Ray Wyatt, Fred Richards was instrumental in getting me invited to speak in two churches in Marion, Indiana. Fred volunteered to lead us to the church around 10 a.m. His sporty Corvette showed up at 9:30. I rolled outside and up to the car. I noticed Fred seemed to be asleep—his eyes were closed. I knocked on the window, startling Fred, and asked, "Are you early or is my watch wrong?" Fred said he came early to pray for John, Ray, and myself. John had given Fred a copy of my book and from that beginning, I found a lasting friend.

At both of the services in Marion, I shared with the congregation some details of the battle of Dong Quang on December 5,1965. That night, we were badly outnumbered. The V C had probed for a few hours to find a weakness in our lines. Second Platoon was given the task of defending an open area devoid of any natural barriers. The enemy chose Second's front as the best place for them to attack. For much of three hours, they poured wave after wave into the area. Fighting was hand to hand and bayonet to bayonet. If Charlie ever breached the line, with their superior numbers, they would have had an unimpeded advance into Echo Company's command post and the rear of First and Third Platoons. Each time it looked as if they would break through, the Marines would throw them back. The heroic action of Second Platoon saved our whole company that night.

I told both congregations that two Hoosiers were members of that special courageous group and both men were in attendance. I introduced John Hollars and Ray Wyatt as the men and asked them to stand. Each church gave them a two minute thunderous applause. Afterward, friends, fellow workers, and even members of their families remarked that they never knew John and Ray were even in combat. The evening service was televised. People all over Marion knew for the first time that honest to goodness heroes had grown up and lived among them for over fifty years.

An event that took place during the morning service has stayed with me to this day. I was signing copies of the book after the message. I observed a neatly dressed, handsome fiftyish-year-old man about ten feet from me in line. He and his wife were holding hands and standing close to each other. I thought, *what a loving couple the way they are holding on to one another.* For some unexplained reason, I glanced down at my feet and noticed they were sticking out too far and maybe some child or older person would trip over them. I wheeled back 6 or 8 inches and continued to greet folks and sign their books. The *loving couple* finally stood in front of us and the wife purchased a book. She asked me to sign it for her husband. He glanced at me with a "far off" look and said, "I was there in 1968. You brought back lots of memories. Keep reminding others about what we went through." I thanked him for his kind words and then greeted the young lady next in line.

She watched for the couple in front of her to walk out the door and then looked down at me. Suddenly tears began to wash down her cheeks. She said in a hushed voice, "That was my dad. Agent Orange blinded him. I am so glad you came and brought attention to men like Dad." We hugged and I promised to do my best to continue. I thought, *I am so glad that I listened to that voice that reminded me to move back.* Her dad seemed so proud that I did not notice his blindness. If he had fallen, I know it would have greatly embarrassed him.

The Purple Heart Medal is awarded to those who were either killed or wounded as a direct result of combat. Three hundred and four thousand (304,000) purple and gold medals with a profile of George Washington were

179

awarded during the Vietnam War. However, so many men returned home with a disorder that still today causes deep rage and a horrifying fear of going to sleep, because the flash backs and dreams are absolutely screaming. There are so many that now have diabetes, men who fathered deformed babies, and thousands, maybe tens of thousands who have suffered from cancer; all from the toxin spray called Agent Orange. All of those heroes who gave so much, many gave all they had, and yet they received little or no recognition. The blind veteran from Marion should have a Purple Heart, as should many of the men just mentioned. I believe their injuries are combat related, just like mine is. Sacrifice to the degree that so many suffered in Vietnam, should be recognized.

In every single place, Vietnam stories flowed. A high ranking officer told of landing in San Francisco after spending 13 months away from his young family. He was greeted with "Go back baby killer" and much worse. His words to me were, " I was greeted by a large group of dirty, stinking, long haired, foul mouthed, mindless college kids, who had no inkling of what I had just been through. The mosquitoes, leaches, huge rats, monsoon rain that lasted for months, horrible living conditions were the best part of Vietnam. Seeing carnage on a scale unimaginable, men younger than those protestors, giving their legs, arms, sight, and lives so that their families back home could be free and safe. Heck, I spent 13 months so those protesting ingrates could be free."

Our servicemen were ordered not to retaliate when accosted by the protesters. Can you imagine if some had fought back? The headlines probably would have been something like, *Unprovoked Soldier Attacks an Innocent College Student!* Those that joined or were drafted and chose to honor their commitment to this country, those that did not flee to Sweden or Canada, seemingly could not win. If the servicemen fought back, they were bullies. If they did nothing, they looked like they didn't believe in what they were fighting for, or maybe they came across as wimps. A few, however, did fight back.

Larry Cook, an Air Force interceptor and code breaker that flew numerous missions over Hanoi in KC 135s was discharged in the summer of 1970. That September, Larry returned to the University of Tennessee to finish work on his degree. Two weeks into the semester, a group of protestors were chanting and making lots of noise in order to draw a crowd. He heard the familiar screams of *war mongers, baby killers, get out* as he walked close by. Suddenly he saw smoke. He realized those idiots were burning the

American flag! Another step brought back the memory of all the friends in his unit that gave their lives for their country. The crew that relieved Larry's when he returned to the States, was shot down over North Vietnam. All the dead members of that band of brothers were just that—Larry's brothers. Another step and tears began to gush down his face. Larry was alone and figured if he shouted anything at the large group, they probably would turn on him. He saw some UT security guards about fifty feet away and knew that their presence meant the protestors had a permit. Also, if he made a scene, the Chancellor would have to dismiss him from school.

One more step and Larry began crying out loud. Suddenly, he turned and began racing toward the burning flag, screaming at top of his voice, "Get out of my way!" He knocked down one student and grabbed the flag, threw it to the ground and stomped out the flames. He picked up Old Glory and as loud as he could, yelled, "You are not going to burn my country's flag. I've seen this flag draped around too many coffins to stand by and do nothing." About that moment, two security guards rushed through the suddenly stunned, but highly agitated crowd, grabbed Larry and dragged him away. A few days later he was summoned to the Chancellor's office. He was told that crowd had been issued a permit and had every right to assemble and protest. He was told, "You and those like you have been fighting and dying for years so all of us, even those protestors can enjoy the great freedoms we have." The official went on, "Confidentially, I agree with what you did, however, if you repeat your actions, I will be forced to dismiss you from school." Larry told the dean that he did not think he could ever stand by and see his country's flag be burned. Thankfully, he did not witness another flag burning protest through graduation day.

At Rocky Point Baptist Church, I told the congregation that, "Vietnam Veterans accomplished everything our country asked of us. We saw almost 60,000 of the best America had to offer, lay down their lives so that others might be free. We were asked to fight a war with one hand and sometimes two, tied behind our backs. Still yet, against a formidable enemy, we never ever lost a battle. President Ronald Reagan said that the Cold War was over because of what the men and women in Vietnam had accomplished. However, instead of being welcomed home as members of the greatest fighting force this world had ever known, so many of my brothers came home to abuse."

After the service, an old high school classmate told us that abuse was every where, not just in the big cities and large universities. He said it happened even in our own town of Morristown. He told about attending

Walters State Community College in 1969 with a Marine by the name of Tony. Tony had stepped on a land mine and lost much of his left leg. He had rehabbed to the point that few could tell he had a artificial leg. In one particular class, the teacher was a "born again" radical. Long hair and beard, typical college hippie protestor type who would sometimes spend the entire class period ranting about the Vietnam War. His students caught on quickly that if they didn't want to discuss that day's topic, ask about the war.

One day a pimply faced 19-year-old stood and began spouting venom that he hoped would thrill the professor. He started, "I can't believe there are so many stupid, brainwashed people willing to blindly follow this criminal government that is so obviously wrong. The dumbest of the lot have to be those men who are being killed every day. They died for no reason. What good can ever come of killing innocent women and children?" Feeling his oats, he ranted on, " Next are the men who are losing body parts. They will spend a life of misery and for what? To brag about killing another baby? One day it will dawn on them that their country lied and tricked them." Smiling retrospectively, he said, " The sad thing is, you and I will have to support them for the remainder of their lives!"

At that moment, the young man felt a thumb and middle finger wrap around the back of his neck. The proper pressure was applied and down to the floor went the kid. Tony then put his artificial leg's boot on mister pimples throat and starred down at him. Tony said, "I gave this leg so that ingrates like you could enjoy freedom of speech, but, I did not give it for you to dishonor my brothers who spilled their blood for this country." He went on, "If I ever hear you disrespect any person who is willing to fight and die for you, next time I'll twist my boot and you'll spend the rest of your time in a wheelchair." Tony raised his foot off of the kid's throat, calmly apologized to the professor and walked out of the class. The young man popped up and ran after Tony. He kept saying, "I'm so sorry, I didn't realize what I was saying, please forgive me." Later, Tony and the kid became good friends.

The best comment about *What a Life* came in the Fall of 2004. We were attending the Battalion Reunion in Beneld, Illinois. Everyone was gathered in the hotel lobby greeting each other. A slim, in shape, neatly dressed man that looked much too young to be a Vietnam Veteran, walked over toward Patty and me. I knew the face, but not the name. The closer he got, the more teary eyed he became. He grabbed my hand and said, "I'm Ron Issac, remember me?" I said, "Doc, great to see you!" We embraced and held onto each other for a long time. Ron said, "I loved the book. I bought four copies.

It helped me more than you'll ever know. For the past 37 years, I've lived my life in a bunker. *What a Life* helped bring me outside. Thank you."

I learned that Ron had a bad dose of Post Traumatic Stress Disorder. He moved 22 times after the war. It was hard to focus and hold onto a job. He felt as if every one had something against him and wanted to sabotage his life. The dreams were unbearable. Like most vets, Ron held it all inside. One giant reason for his survival, he like me, married up— to an angel. Judi was always there refusing to allow him to give up. Doc Issac, like so many other Corpsmen, saw the very worst of battle, the vicious horror of man's inhumanity to man. There probably aren't any statistics to back this up, but I believe Corpsmen serving in combat are much more likely to have PTSD.

I wrote briefly about Ron in chapter one. During the night battle at the French fort, when the VC began breaking through our lines, a Viet Cong thrust his bayonet into Ron's groin, causing excruciating pain. Doc had given his last dose of morphine to a Marine named Richard Hendrix who had also received a gut wound. It was hours before Ron got some relief. He should have passed out. He was one tough man that all of us admired and cared about. Before joining the Marines as a Corpsman, Ron was a Navy Seal.

General Bill Weise, who is one of the founding fathers of the battalion association brought a good friend of his to the reunion. The friend and I did not speak until the last night, but there was just something there that made me want to talk with her. Signing a book for the General finally got the two of us together. She asked me if there was ever a time when I could not move my arms. That gave me an opportunity to share about the miracle that I received on the day I got hurt. She later revealed the reason for her question. Her son at the age of seventeen was severely injured in an accident and was a quadriplegic for 21 years. He had just recently passed away. She said he told her so many times, "Mama, I could stand being paralyzed and spend the rest of my life in a wheelchair if I could only move my hands."

Each time I visit the Spinal Cord Center at the Veterans Hospital, I feel blessed. Probably seventy per cent of the patients there can not use their hands. On that last night of the reunion, that special mother's question reminded me that I was doubly blessed to be granted that awesome miracle on March 21, 1966.

At the reunion banquet, we sat with Ed Brummett, John and Kay Hollars, and Ray and Suzi Wyatt. Ed brought in a paper bag wrapped around something. People were coming by and asking, "What's in the bag, Ed?" Ed kept joking, "It's none of your business, or it's my supper." The guys had visited Vietnam with General Brown the previous May on a military sponsored tour. I was invited to go, and really wanted to, but knew a third world country would be anything but wheelchair friendly. At the table, we discussed their trip. After the guest speaker finished, the 2-4 President, Jack Petrowski invited Ed to come up and say something about their trip to Nam.

Ed began by inviting me to come up to the front. Ed had that bag with him. He said, "As most of you know, General Brown wanted to be here tonight and make this presentation, but is still back in Florida recovering from surgery." He turned toward me and said, "Randy, we visited the battleground just west of the Phoung Dinh village complex in the Vinh Tuy valley. The General walked over to a spot and reflectively paused. He then bent over and picked up a smooth rock and told us that was the exact location where he lost his radioman on March 21, 1966. We members of Echo Company had that rock mounted on a piece of marble from Marble Mountain and inscribed with these words: Lance Corporal Randy Kington—2nd Battalion 4th Marines— Phoung Dinh 2 Vietnam— March 21 1966." I was given the plaque and asked to say a few words. I was overwhelmed. I uttered something, but spent most of my effort trying not to break down in front of all of those Marines. What a group of friends God has blessed me with.

One of the last Morristown churches I spoke in before returning to Naples was Russellville Baptist. The pastor, Steve Smith invited us to have lunch after church with his family. I asked, "Pastor, I'm curious. How did you hear about us?" He replied, " Richard Emmert told me I could not go wrong if you would speak for Russellville." I had heard that if a pastor recommended a guest speaker to another minister, that minister in turn would likely reciprocate by recommending someone to speak for the other pastor. For that reason, we had not imposed on Dr. Emmert for recommendations. He took it upon himself to see that churches in the area invited us to share our testimony. Richard is not only a great pastor, but a great friend.

Russellville Baptist was the only church that Patty was not able to attend with me in 2004. My oldest son Johnny was present and took care of the books after the service. In both the early and the 10:45 a.m. service, I shared how complete Patty had made my life. I told them about Patty giving up her dream of having a career in medicine in order to be my wife. From the time she was in grade school, Patty wanted to make a difference. Instead of helping thousands of sick and injured people get better, Patty gave up her dream, actually her life, and for the past 38 years, she has been pouring her selfless love, her healing into one broken Vietnam Veteran and making my life more complete. I brought a large framed picture of Patty and placed it in the entrance of the church. Most stopped at the picture to view what a real angel looked like before greeting Johnny and me. So many times afterward, people would come up to Patty in town and introduce themselves as attending church in Russellville and were thrilled to finally meet in person Randy Kington's angel.

The most unique church we spoke in was the Naples Community Church. The congregation meets in the downtown park called Cambier Park. At the spring book signing on Fifth Avenue, a military buff by the name of Sherman Collins invited me to come over to his home and browse through his collection. The vast amount and quality of memorabilia Sherman had was mind boggling. His wife Sherry mentioned that she had read *What a Life* and invited Patty and me over for supper. At the meal, the Collins said they wanted us to meet their pastor, Dr. Gene Scott. Dr. Scott a few years back, began delivering sermons from a park bandstand. There are so many condos and guest rooms within walking distance, he believed a church in the park would be an excellent way to reach out. Soon the services were packed. Amazingly, in over five years, there has been only one service canceled because of rain. This past spring (2005) as many as 4,000 people attended one of their services.

Dr. Scott invited me to speak at their Veterans Day program. I put on my best blue suit, white shirt, and flag tie. We arrived at the park early in order to find a parking space. The pastor came running out to the car to offer assistance. I turned to Patty and asked, "What's wrong with this picture?" Gene had on a pair of Bermuda shorts and a Hawaiian shirt. He grinned and said, "Didn't I tell you, our services are very laid back?" Talk about being over dressed, I was the only person there in a suit. The Marine honor guard from the Naples Marine Corps League detachment participated in the program. The Commandant of the group, Gary Shannanbarger, played "Taps" and brought the—started to say house—park down. Many of our Florida neighbors attended as did many Marine friends. I spoke on the topic, *Do Not Forget*. I believe there were at least four members there who were Korean War veterans of the Chosin Reservoir battle. I spoke of their sacrifice and encouraged everyone to never forget those heroes, and *all* who have given so much in order that Americans everywhere might be free.

Gary Brown called and said he wanted to attend the 2004 Naples Marine

Corps Ball. Said he enjoyed the last one so much. Ed Brummett, Tom Gardner, and Ed Martin called that Fall and also wanted to come. Driving down from Tennessee, Patty and I talked about the new friends we had made since meeting Gary, and how much we were looking forward to being with them again. One of us brought up the award (text is at the end of General Brown's foreword at the beginning of the book) the General had recommended the Marine Corps grant me. It had been requested two years prior and I had assumed it had just been filed away. I told Patty, "It would be such a great privilege to be recognized, but just knowing Gary Brown feels like I deserve that award is more than enough of an honor." Patty grinned as if she knew something I didn't, then said, "I feel the same way."

Far left, Commandant Gary Shanabarger is reading my Bronze Star Citation. Next is General Gary Brown, Patty, me, Third Platoon Sergeant Ed Brummitt, Corpsman "Doc" Ed Martin, and Fireteam Leader "Top Cat" Tom Gardner.

The 2004 Marine Corps Ball was the most special one I have ever attended. After the guest speaker finished, the detachment Commandant invited General Brown to read a note from the current Marine Corps Commandant, General Michael Hagee. A Call to Order was sounded and all the Marines in the room stood at attention. Then the General invited Patty and me to appear to his front. The Commandant directed General Brown to award me a Bronze Star for action taken during hostile action on March 21, 1966. The letter directed the presentation to be at a place deemed appropriate. I could not have chosen a better setting. My Platoon Commander, Sgt. Brummett, Doc Martin, Top Cat, and all the Naples Marines shared in one of my proudest moments. General Brown was asked to speak for the television cameras. He said the nicest things about his former radio operator. He had to leave immediately after the Ball for Jacksonville, a good six hours away. I really felt honored that he would put so much effort into recognizing me. In Vietnam, then Lt. Brown was my commander, my boss. In the Marines, the enlisted and officers are supposed to keep their distance in order to better maintain discipline. Even at a distance, all of Third Platoon admired and respected him. We would follow him anywhere. However, the past three years, he and I have become good friends. No one could ask for a better friend than Gary Brown. I thought, *What a life I have lived, and it just keeps getting better!*

The winter in Naples was a great time for us. Still, the churches were reluctant to have me speak. A few did. The pastor at Marco Island First Baptist, Tim Neptune, invited me to return and share more of my story. Mostly we were asked to speak in civic groups like the Rotaries and Kiwanis. After the civic programs, there was usually a question and answer time. Even after the election, the most common questions had to do with John Kerry. *What do you think about the Purple Hearts and the Silver Star that many are questioning, his protesting the war and calling the veterans war criminals, lying about throwing away his medals, etc.?* My response was generally, "I forgave John Kerry and Jane Fonda a long time ago. They wanted the same thing I did, for the war to end. However, I believe they went about it the wrong way. I believe lives were lost because of their actions. But, that was over 30 years ago and now, I believe the country wants to put the division behind us and heal." I went on, "Today, we have men and women in harm's way in Iraq and Afghanistan. Whether one supports the action or not, we have to support the troops. I hope we learned a valuable lesson in the 60s and early 70s. Never can we allow a few to disrespect American servicemen to the degree the Vietnam Veterans were mistreated. Men and women in our armed forces are just doing what we all want them to do—protect us."

In February, I was invited to attend a fancy fund raiser with General Brown and the Naples Marine Corps League. Tom Monahan, who served in the Marine Corps in the 50's and is the founder of Dominos Pizza, threw a party to raise money for scholarships for dependents of Marines. Mr. Monahan and the Collier family are building a new Catholic University in Collier County, Florida. Ava Maria will one day rival Notre Dame. The guest speaker and former Commandant of the Corps, General Charles Krulak, walked over and said, "Randy, I loved your book!" It had been forty years ago at Camp Pendleton that I last saw the General, who was then a 2nd Lt.. It was a tremendous honor that he would take the time to read *What A Life.*

General Gary Brown, me, and General Charles Krulak at the Gyrene Gala, February 11, 2005.

There were two Medal of Honor recipients at the event called The Gyrene Gala. Both were Vietnam Veterans that Gary knew personally. Barney Barnum, who retired a Colonel, stayed with Gary and me for quite a while, sharing story after story. The other holder of this country's highest military honor, Major General James Livingston, was the Company Commander of Echo Co., my old outfit, in 1967. I shared a story with him that showed the high character this man possesses.

Two sisters, Nancy Henson and Beverly Nelson moved into our Tennessee neighborhood a couple of years back. One brought her spouse Jack, the other, memories of her husband. Don Nelson was a Vietnam Veteran who was very proud to have served his country as a Marine. His pride of the Corps was such that he wanted to be buried in his dress blues. He spent much of his last months hospitalized or at home under the care of hospice with an agonizingly painful form of cancer caused from Agent Orange.

Beverly and I became good friends. She told me a Marine General and her husband visited together one day at the hospital. Then, later on, this General would come by, pull up a chair and just talk with Don. "We had never met this special Marine before the visits. It really lifted Don's spirits to have such an important man show so much genuine concern for him." She went on, "Did I tell you this General had received the Congressional Medal Of Honor?"

I asked the General, "That was you, wasn't it, Sir?"

General Livingston looked away and said, "Yes, he was one of mine."

In March, 2005, Homer Helter invited me to meet a good friend of his, Lt. General Hal Moore. General Moore wrote the best seller *We Were Soldiers Once ...and Young* that was made into a movie starring Mel Gibson. The picture is the only Vietnam movie in my opinion that comes close to being real. I was grateful to meet this American hero. General Moore, age 83, spoke to the group of us for an hour an half, non stop.

He asked me what outfit I served with. "Echo Company, 2nd Battalion, 4th Marines, Sir." I answered.

He replied," I remember you guys. We were to push the enemy from II Corps into you on Operation Double Eagle."

I agreed, "That's right, Sir. I remember that time well." I wrote about the Operation in Chapter 8, but I read old letters to jog my memory. After 39 years, this 83-year-old man remembered off the cuff.

The last thing I said was, "General, you would have made a great Marine officer." His smile said, "I was even prouder to be an Air Calvary officer, but thanks for the compliment. "

We came back to Tennessee early; my biggest fan was sick. Mom had a form of blood cancer and it suddenly began to get serious. We spent seven quality weeks with her before she passed away on June 12, 2005. I told someone the other day that I had spent most of my life trying to convince others and myself that I was not a mama's boy. How wrong I was. There is a special bond between a son and mother that is unlike any other. I have a huge hole in my heart that I am hoping time will someday heal.

Bob and Deola Kington, the best parents any son could ever have.

Going through Mom's belongings made me both sad and proud. She kept everything that was associated with me, even little things like a plastic car. My sisters used to joke with her, "Mom, we know who is number one, but which one of us is second?" She never needed an excuse to bring up my name, however, *What a Life* gave her more opportunities. She carried a copy with her to the store, beauty shop, church, Senior Citizens, everywhere. I lost count how many books that lady sold. She loved emailing, even strangers. Two weeks before Mom died, I mailed two books to people who had learned of me from her emails.

The church in Marion, Indiana, had made a nice poster to advertise the Sunday service I was speaking in. I brought Mom one back. Sometime in March 2005, she placed the poster in a frame, stood it on the dining table, and laid two books in front. Laughing, Vicki asked, "Mama, I see you have made a shrine to Randy." She replied, "No, there are so many nurses, therapists, and visitors coming by, I thought they would want one of Randy's books." When Mom slipped into a coma, one of the hospice nurse's daughter asked for a copy. I was pleased to sign it. Even near death, my proud mother was still selling my books.

The summer and fall of 2005 were loaded with speaking engagements. We began traveling farther and farther away from Morristown. Louisville, Ky., Roanoke, Va., Cartersville, Ga., all over East TN., are just a few of the places. No matter the location, the Vietnam stories were the same. I never dreamed so many people were still hurting after all these years. I read on the internet that Vietnam Vets had fewer problems than most other war vets. I don't know where that came from. Maybe the statistics that were quoted did not take into account the number of Vietnam Vets that won't talk about their problems, that hold it all inside. All the families of veterans that reported the past two years about their loved ones' pain and suffering is staggering. Just extrapolating from the few places we have visited, hundreds of thousands of Vietnam Veterans are still being impacted from what happened over thirty some years ago.

I was watching a program about Vietnam on the History Channel two years ago. It reported that the average World War II veteran spent an average of forty days in combat for the period of Dec. 7, 1941, to Sept. 2, 1945. The average Vietnam Vet spent an average of 250 days in combat for each thirteen month tour of duty. The helicopter and advanced mobility coupled with the fact that there were no real front or rear lines, made conflict a daily fact of life. I thought after seeing the program, *No wonder so many of our guys are still hurting. Eighteen and 19-year-olds should never have seen what we saw, but to see the horror over and over. . .*

A reporter for the Greeneville Sun, Bob Hurley, wrote a neat 2005 Fourth of July article about Patty and me. Bob asked, "Why don't you wear your dress blues when you speak?"

I replied, "I'm 58 years old. I don't want people to think I am trying to be someone that I'm not. I don't want them thinking I am there for a show."

"No one will think that," Bob said. "Actually, I believe more doors will be opened for you and people will listen more attentively to what you have to say."

I thought long and hard about wearing my uniform. I am awfully proud of my country and the time I was able to serve in her armed forces. I love to be described as a patriot, and wearing those dress blues seems to demonstrate just how much I love America. But even more, if it caused just one person to listen more attentively, it would be worth it. The Good Book states, "We are saved by hearing the Word." In the messages I deliver, I use Scripture. I began wearing my uniform in August, 2005. The first six Sundays, 32 people invited Jesus Christ to be their Lord and Savior. Was it the uniform? Probably not, but from now on, I believe I'll wear it.

Outside the Victory Church of God in Greeneville, TN. on August 7, 2005.

Almost every place we speak, both of us are showered with thanks and appreciation for being there. One night after church, I asked Patty, "What did I say that would cause such a response?"

Patty answered, " I believe so many people were affected by Vietnam. I don't think it is so much the words you used. Seeing you, and hearing what happened to you probably reminds them that after such long a time they haven't been totally forgotten."

Honestly, I don't know why we have been received so well and the response has been so great. What ever it is, I look forward to it lasting for a long time. I told one audience, "Many have described *What a Life* as a healing book; I know it was healing for me to write it." I hope these past two years traveling about the country and sharing my story, have been healing for the listeners. I know it has been just that for me.

What a life God has blessed me with.

Front is granddaughter Gentry, from left to right are son Johnny, wife Ana, son Josh, grandson Joshua, me, and Patty

Epilogue

What a wonderful life I have lived. The major defining moments of Randy Kington are:

Parris Island where I became a man,
Serving with Gary Brown and Echo Company in Vietnam,
The injury on 3-21-1966,
God saving my life and soul,
God giving me back my hands,
Meeting and marrying Patty,
Conference with Dr. Edward Spatz.

My first seventeen years were years of which I am not proud. Reviewing, they probably were not any worse than anyone else's, but I am disappointed at all the opportunities I missed to make something out of myself. Sometime after my twelfth birthday, I began to exert my independence at the expense of doing what was right. Maybe rebellion is a more descriptive word for it. I did not totally right my ship until Operation Texas. I did, however, take some giant steps toward being the person I wanted to be at Parris Island. Even at such a young age, I was transformed into a man on that island. For the first time in my life I could look myself in the mirror and like what I saw. I learned valuable lessons there such as honor, duty, love of country, discipline, and putting the team ahead of the individual. And I loved those dress blues and the tradition woven into their fabric.

Vietnam taught me to appreciate the awesome blessings we enjoy as Americans. I saw poverty in the Philippines and Hong Kong, but the South Vietnamese were not only poor, they had little chance of being anything else. Serving with and fighting alongside members of Echo Company, Second Battalion, Fourth Marines was one of my greatest honors. First Lieutenant Gary Brown taught me how to conduct myself as a man. He had a management style that demanded my best. He didn't rant and rave, scream, or get abusive. He led by example and rarely had to raise his voice. He cared about those who were under his command. He took his office and leadership role seriously. He was always under control and he convinced me if I followed his orders, I would come back home alive. He was right. If he had not killed the VC who shot me and then had the guys quickly move me to safety, I would surely have been killed. His style made me want to do my best even when he was not around. Management 301 at Carson Newman was old hat because I had already been through the book with Gary Brown. When I found myself in leadership positions over the years, I used the example Gary had demonstrated thirty-six years ago as my guide

March 21, 1966, saw a healthy, robust, six foot two inch, 190 pounder with a thirty inch waist devolve into someone physically lacking much. My arms never stopped hurting, but that is the only problem I now have. I never have a headache and my upper body is stronger than most other fifty-six-year-olds. Living in Florida with its warmth has really made a difference. Life hasn't always been perfect. Over the past thirty-seven years I've had eight paraplegia-related surgeries, cancer, broken bones and more. Physically, I'm not the man I once was, but I am light years ahead of that nineteen-year-old. I am totally self sufficient, able to live alone if necessary. I weigh 185, which is five pounds less than my weight at age nineteen, but my waist has grown some.

I haven't allowed the wheelchair to slow me except for the obvious barriers such as steps and curbs. We used to travel a lot, even to Europe once. I still drive my own car. People still stare, and little kids are forever asking, "Why can't he walk?" but it really doesn't bother me anymore. I am very proud that many people say, "After being with you for a few minutes, I forget you are in a wheelchair." I want my chair to be somewhat like a good referee. When you think of a great basketball game, you don't remember the referee, even though he is a necessary part of the game. When you meet me, I want you to remember me, not my wheelchair, even though it is a necessary part of my life.

The most outstanding moment of my life was accepting Christ as my personal Savior. It is still difficult for me to understand why the Creator of the universe would take the time to save my life, save my soul, and return my hands to me. Lou Gehrig once told a capacity crowd at Yankee stadium, he was the luckiest man ever. Lou didn't know Randy Kington, or he would have claimed second place. The peace of knowing that my future is secure and I will spend eternity in heaven far outweighs any physical difficulties I may experience. I do not have a choice, but if I did, I would not trade my life now for the one I had before 3-21-1966.

Having my arms and hands returned to me was major. With my hands, I can drive, transfer in and out of the chair, and a host of other things. Having my hands allows Patty to be my wife fulltime and not a total caregiver. I'm not sure I am strong enough to be a quadriplegic. Thanks to God, I'll never know the agony of having lost the use of both my arms and legs.

I have certainly been blessed. I have not experienced the flash backs and nightmares that many other Vietnam veterans have. I believe when God saved me, He also gave me the ability to cope with being hurt. There have been some medical setbacks over the years, but He has given me the ability to handle all of them. After I was first injured, I am sure depression was a part of my life, especially for the first five months after leaving Memphis. I did not feel sorry for myself, but I did stay "down." Patty saved my life. She gave me something to live for. I wanted to be the type of person she deserved, knowing as much as I tried I would fail. She is an extraordinary person. For thirty-six years she has looked past my shortcomings and treated me as her best friend. So far, no sacrifice has been too much. Little things, for example, at eating functions, I have to use both hands to push the wheelchair and can't hold a plate and move the chair at the same time. Patty gets my plate and then usually goes back to the end of the line for hers. No computer has enough memory to record all the sacrifices she has made for me. The other day, Patty was telling a friend how much she admired me and the sacrifices she thought I had made. She was told, "Patty, I admire you just as much. Randy didn't have a choice in his sacrifice, you did." Truly God gave me one of his best!

Lastly, the meeting with Dr. Spatz encouraged me to get on with the rest of my life. I prayed every day for God to heal me, but after the Boston meeting I realized I wasn't going to have that prayer answered. My future revolved around me getting my feeling back and walking again. I wanted to be an operator of heavy equipment, and that required healthy legs. I couldn't admit to others and myself that I would spend the rest of my life in a wheelchair. I really didn't want to face that prospect and deep down hoped that one morning I just wouldn't wake up. I loved Patty but thought she would be much better off without me. But after hearing I was a miracle from Dr. Spatz and how fortunate I was that I could use my hands, eventually I decided to make the most of what I'd been given.

Probably even more than our Boston meeting, the love and confidence of Patty made me want to try as much as possible to be all I could be. Actually, for the last thirty-six years, I have wanted to repay her for making my life complete, and have Patty be proud of me. What a great life mine continues to be!

Appendix

Memorial Day, July the Fourth and Veterans Day Message

By Randy Kington

INTRODUCTION

I wrote a book about my life and called it *What a Life.* God has used the book to open so many doors for me to share Jesus Christ with others. In churches, colleges, and so many different groups, each place, God seems to greatly bless. To think, the seed that grew into *What a Life* was planted on a holiday just like this one—Memorial Day, 1999, in a VA hospital. More about that later.

SCRIPTURE

Deuteronomy : Chapter 6, verse 12
Then beware lest you forget the Lord, which brought you forth out of the land of Egypt.

PRAYER
TEXT

It was important to God that the Children of Israel not forget how they got to the Promised Land. It was important they remembered the parting of the Red Sea, the manna from heaven, the leaders like Moses, Aaron, and Joshua, and crossing the River Jordan. One of the first acts the people were commanded to do after arriving in the land of Milk and Honey, was to build an altar of twelve stones so that generations after would always remember.

On this special day, I believe God would be pleased if we remember how America became our promised land. We should never forget that the greatness of these United States, down through the years, has always rested on the sacrifices of so many. Those sacrifices were made for you and me. Because of those sacrifices, this nation is free today.

On March 21st, 1966, a North Vietnamese bullet tore into my neck, touching the spinal cord, and paralyzing me for the rest of my life. Now, please don't feel sorry for me. I met Jesus Christ while that round found its way into my back. The impact of that 7.62 millimeter round lifted me up off of a rice paddy dike, into the air, and once in the air, I could not come back down. I began to float over the battlefield in slow motion. My first thought was, *I'm going to die, or maybe I'm already dead and I've used up all of my chances to be right with God.* I knew exactly where I was headed and it scarred the daylights out of me. I screamed from the bottom of my soul, "Please Lord, don't let my mother bury me; she can't handle that. Please Lord, save my soul." He answered my cry!

The moment that warmth of grace and mercy began flowing into my heart, I fell to the ground. I landed on my back so hard, that my knees flew up into my face, causing my ammo belt to squeeze into my diaphragm so tightly that I was unable to pull any air into my lungs—not any at all. I tried to get up and could not. I ordered my hands to lift and they didn't work; I didn't feel them. Unable to move or breath, I didn't panic. I calmly rolled my eyes toward the sky and asked, "God, I need my arms, please." Before I got the word please out, feeling rushed into my shoulders and down into my fingers. I quickly moved my legs off my face and took in one of the sweetest breaths of air I had ever experienced. I had been a Christian for less than a minute and Almighty God was already answering prayer. What a life! What a God!

One March day, God saved my life and then gave me a miracle so enormous that words just aren't adequate to describe. However, saving my soul was the greatest thing He did for me. Because of that moment, I now have a home in heaven awaiting me. I am going to spend eternity there. After hearing that, how can anyone feel sorry for me?

Because of the severity of my injury, I spent the next nine months in hospitals all across the States. One of the many things I learned was, if one had to be in a military or VA hospital, the best times were Memorial Day, July 4th, or Veterans Day. There was always a parade on those days, a barbeque or fish fry, and many times a high ranking officer would come by and tell us how appreciative this country was of our sacrifice. It was a really feel good time.

In 1999, I had an occasion to visit the huge VA Medical Center in Augusta, Georgia. I was given a few dates from which to choose. I chose Memorial Day. I woke up on that holiday morning and there was a nurse in my room. I asked, "What time do all the fun events begin?"

She turned toward me and replied, "According to the morning report Mr. Kington, there is nothing special planned for you men today."

Astonished, I asked, "On Memorial Day?" She nodded.

That afternoon, I was alone, having a heated conversation with myself. *America, how could you not remember! If a hospital for veterans forgets, what is the rest of the country doing?* I thought back to all the local military parades down Main Street when I first came back home to Morristown. We haven't had one in years; there is just not enough interest. When my sons were in school, they got out for Labor Day and a host of other holidays, but were always in attendance on the last Monday of May, the day we honor those who have sacrificed their all for our country.

Then the thought passed by, *before you become too indignant, what have you done to remember?* I then saw the face of Navy Corpsman, Gary Hann. For years, I had meant to call Gary's parents and let them know what a hero their son was on the day I was shot. Gary was attached to our Battalion. He was with us when we assaulted a village holding as many as 1500 North Vietnamese troops. Echo Company began the battle with only 157 men, and in no time 95 young Marines had fallen. Amidst the falling mortar rounds and blistering machine gun fire, Gary, with little regard for his own safety, ran to fallen comrades, administering what medical help he could. Suddenly, a voice about thirty feet to his front, screamed, "Doc, I'm hit real bad, help!" Gary grabbed his medical bag and quickly ran toward the fallen voice. Into his third step, an enemy bullet found him and ended twenty-year-old Gary Hann's life.

When I returned home, one of the first things I did was pick up the phone and call Gary's hometown of Ausmus, Oregon. I learned that there were no Hanns living there anymore. I spoke to the librarian who didn't have any information on Gary Hann. The 75-year-old town historian didn't remember that Gary had died during the Vietnam War.

I thought, *I may be the only person in the world who remembers Doc Hann.* The Cherokee Indians have a belief that one is never really dead as long as one person still remembers them. I determined to never forget Navy Corpsman, Gary Hann. I also determined to never forget all of those who down through the years have suffered and sacrificed for this country.

It is easy to remember the brave young men and women in Afghanistan and Iraq, but I want to remember even those from the very beginning of the founding of this country.

I don't want to ever forget the men at Valley Forge, where our troops wintered with General Washington. It was so cold and our men were so under supplied that many did not even have shoes. Over 300 American soldiers had their feet amputated because of frostbite suffered during that encampment. I'll never forget those men.

The Marines who stormed the Halls of Montezuma in Mexico City, where the carnage was so great, it was reported that blood ran down the street ankle deep. I'll never forget those brave men.

Gettysburg, San Juan Hill, the rat infested muddy trenches of World War I, and the sixteen million men and women who saved the world from tyranny in places like Tarrawa, Iwo Jima, and Normandy. Very few of those members of the greatest generation are still with us. I'll never forget those to whom so much is owed.

During the winter, I have the privilege of having lunch each Wednesday with a group of retired Marines. Many in the group are Korean War Veterans who fought in a place called the Chosin Resevoir. For two weeks, in temperatures that hovered around forty degrees below zero, they found themselves surrounded by twelve Chinese divisions. Headlines all across America reported, ***First Marine Division About to Surrender or be Annihilated***. Neither happened. In what turned out to be one of this country's greatest victories, the Marines broke out of the trap and in doing so, totally destroyed six of those enemy divisions. But for 54 years, the surviors of the Chosin Campaign have suffered excruciating and debilitating pain in their limbs and joints. I'll never forget those heroes.

And those who fought in Vietnam where almost 60,000 of this countries finest, laid down their lives. I brought my Purple Heart and will set it on a table outside if you would like to see it. Three hundred and four thousand of these medals were awarded during the Vietnam War. However, so many of those who were hurt the most, never received this award. Many brought home a disorder that still today causes deep rage and a horrifying fear of falling asleep, because the dreams and nightmares are absolutely screaming. It is hard for them to focus and hold a job. Sadly, many have ended their own lives thinking that is the only way to escape. One hundred and seventy-seven thousand Vietnam Veterans have, or soon will have, type two diabetes caused by a defoliant called Agent Orange. Many men came home and fathered deformed babies because of that poison. And tens of thousands down through the years have died slow and painful deaths due to Agent Orange cancer. All the missing limbs, faces, and wheelchairs that returned home. It has been almost 40 years and still, so many Vietnam Veterans are hurting. But, I learned that their deepest pain goes so much farther than physical injury.

We did everything our country asked of us and then some. We were asked to fight a war with one hand tied behind our backs, and still yet, we never lost a battle. Instead of being welcomed home and recognized as members of the greatest fighting force this world had ever known, so many of my brothers returned home to abuse. They were literally spit on, waste was thrown on them, the protestors screamed at them and called them the vilest of names. And down through the years, these men rarely hear anything positive about the time they served this great country, about the time they were willing to lay down their lives, so that others might be free. I'll never forget those who gave so much and were appreciated so little.

For the past 229 years, over one million members of our armed forces have given their lives on behalf of this country. Many more have incurred injuries, some causing a lifetime of suffering. For what? To make sure we remain a free nation. Join me on this special day in rememberance of all of those who have given so much.

Today I would like to recognize another group of great patriots, people who rarely receive recognition. These folks never receive medals of valour, yet they are some of the bravest and most courageous people you and I know. They have never been awarded a Purple Heart, yet they have suffered and sacrificed greatly for this country. I'm refering to family members.

During WWII, families were encouraged to place a blue star in their front window, one for each son, dad, or husband serving in our military.

Those stars were placed with much pride, also much trepedation. In the event a loved one was killed in service, the blue star was replaced with a gold one. Three hundred and ninety-one thousand gold stars dotted front windows all across America. Many homes had more than one gold star displayed. The Sullivan family in Waterloo, Iowa had five. I can not even begin to imagine the pain and suffering those families experienced, especially on the day that dreaded telegram arrived. The one that began, "We regret to inform you . . ."

And those families that welcomed home broken bodies from wars. I am an eye wittness that families suffer as much or more than even those who were injured. An olive green Dodge sedan pulled up into my parents' driveway on March 22, 1966. A Marine Captain came to the front door carrying a telegram that told of my condition. My Mom saw the telegram, thought I was dead, and immediately had a breakdown from which she never really recovered. My Dad grieved for his only son till the day he died six years ago. My two sons grew into manhood without the help of a whole father; without the same growing their grandfather had invested in me.

And my beautiful wife Patty. For over 38 years, Patty has been sacrificing on my behalf. From the moment we met, Patty seemed to be on a mission. She was willing to pay any price, make any sacrifice in order that I not fail. Early in our marriage, Patty recognized that I would never be a contributor; not until I learned how to respect myself again. She said, "You need to go back to school."

"But, Patty, it's been almost five years, I don't have the confidence anymore, and what will people say when I fell?"

Patty said, "I won't let you fail. I'll take every class you take. I'll type your papers, take notes—I'll make sure you have the tools to get through." For five long years, Patty took boring accounting classes, just to make sure I succeeded. And I might add, she graduated with honors in a curriculum in which she had little or no interest. For the past 14,000 plus days, Patty has been sacrificing on my behalf. So much so, that huge computer down in Oak Ridge doesn't have the capacity to count even half of them. In Vietnam, I was surrounded by some of this nation's bravest men and down through the years, I have been privileged to meet some of this country's most highly decorated veterans, even Medal of Honor recipients. But, Patty Lois Barber Kington is the bravest, most courageous, selfless loving person I have ever encountered.

Thank you Patty. I'll never forget you. Today, I ask all of you to join me in never forgetting all of the millions of Pattys, who for 229 years, have been suffering and sacrificing on behalf of our great country.

Finally, I will never forget my Heavenly Father. Our nation is the greatest country on the face of this planet, only because of the will and grace of God. The President recently said, "Freedom is a gift from the Almighty." I believe that because the Bible says, *All good things come from God.* I believe it was God who placed on the hearts of Thomas Jefferson and the other framers, the concepts of liberty, justice and freedom. I believe it was the Lord who on July 4, 1776, gave our brave forefathers the courage and wisdom it took for them to make that stand against wrong. Because they stood tall, we have since been, *One nation, under God, indivisible, with liberty and justice for all!*

In the book of Psalms, we are told that before any of us were born, God prepared a special work for each of us. I believe there are few works more special than the *work* of defending one's country. Of protecting our brothers and sisters from the evils of the Hitlers of this world. For 229 years, He has been preparing the very best this country has to offer for just such a *work.* Since 1776, He has been instilling in our young defenders, honor, duty, disipline, courage, and even love. Those qualities were found in Medal of Honor recipient Elbert Kinser, who grew up a few miles from my home.

On Okinawa, a Japanese granade landed in the middle of Elbert's platoon. Twenty-three-year-old Sergeant Kinser dove on the grenade, smothered it with his body, and allowed it to blow up into him, saving the lives of all of his men. Two thousand years ago, Jesus Christ recognized Elbert Kinser, and I believe the millions more who down through the years, have been willing to give their lives for this noble country. Jesus said, "There is no greater love than the love a man has that would cause him to lay down his life for a friend."

Today we have been singing and talking about freedom and sacrifice. I don't have to remind you, the greatest sacrifice was when our Heavenly Father allowed a mob of ungrateful, selfish, angry people, to mistreat, abuse, torture, and even kill His only begotten Son—just so we would know the true meaning of freedom; to be free from sin, to be free to worship our Heavenly Father, and to be free to spend eternity in heaven with the Father, the Son, and the Holy Spirit.

I will never forget that God truly did shed His grace on the United States of America.

CONCLUSION

William Barclay wrote about a young French Soldier during World War I. The seventeen-year-old sustained a nasty shrapnel wound to his upper right arm. He was brought to the surgeon's tent by his comrades. This soldier was the eptimony of life's best offering. He was very handsome, his body athletic and taut, and he spoke with such clarity and intelligence. Everyone in the tent just knew this young man's future was as bright as the noonday sun.

The surgeons began working on his mangled arm, and tried with all of their might to piece the shattered bones and ligaments together again. In the end, the arm had to be taken, three inches below the shoulder blade.

One of the doctors spoke up, "I am going to stay with this soldier until he awakens. I fear when he sees his missing arm, he will believe his life to be over and may go into shock."

Later, in recovery, the seventeen-year-old began moving around cautiously and then, he barely opened his eyes. At that moment, the doctor grabbed the youngster's left hand and apologetically said, "I am so sorry. We tried with all of our might to repair your limb, but in the end, your arm was taken."

The young soldier, by now fully awake, faced toward the doctor and respectfully replied, "Sir, you did not *take* my arm. I *gave* my arm for my country!"

Reading about that patriot, I thought about all of those servicemen who since 1776 have given so much. Yesterday, two gave all they had. I thought of all the families who have suffered so much. And I thought of my Heavenly Father who sacrificed His Son for us. I reflected, *if only there were some way to speak to those to whom so much is owed. If we could corporately let them know how sorry we are that so much was taken from them.* I believe their reply would be similar to the French soldier's, *"You did not take anything from me. I gave so that you might be free."*

Freedom and sacrifice have always gone together. Resolve with me today to never forget those whose sacrifices are the very reason we are free. May God continue to bless The United States of America.

The United States Marine Corps Hymn

From the Halls of Montezuma
To the shores of Tripoli;
We will fight our country's battles
In the air, on land, and sea;
First to fight for right and freedom
And to keep our honor clean;
We are proud to claim the title
Of United States Marines.
Our flag's unfurl'd to ev'ry breeze
From dawn to setting sun;
We have fought in ev'ry clime and place
Where we could take a gun;
In the snow of far off northern lands
And sunny tropic scenes;
You will always find us on the job—
The United States Marines.
Here's health to you and to our corps
Which we are proud to serve;
In many a strife we've fought for life
And never lost our nerve;
If the Army or the Navy
Ever look on Heaven's scenes;
They will find the streets are guarded
By United States Marines.

Tribute to a Corpsman

While serving with the Fleet Marines in the hell of mortal combat,
There huddled in a foxhole, a waiting Corpsman sat.

Softly he whispered as he looked to the skies,
God give me the courage to answer their cries.

Then came the cry he was trained to hear,
He knew he must run fast and cast away his fear.
Up and out of the foxhole, and moving like a deer,
The cries for help grew louder so he knew he must be near.

Finally he reached the man and ran swiftly to his side,
The man was in agony, but thanking God that he hadn't died.

Quickly and with much care the Corpsman gave first aid,
As shells exploded all around them; close to where they laid.

Then he moved on down the line to aid others in distress,
Never taking a moment's time to stop and rest.

From man to man he made his way, through the rain of enemy fire,
In and out of foxholes and through barbed wire, he made his way.

In and out of the enemies' vicious fire, until a bullet shot through the air
And struck him in the back; then suddenly the skies were filled with the
brightness of the sun,
So he knew that God was proud of the job that he had done.
He closed his eyes; after which he knew no more.

He had served with honor as a member of the Hospital Corps.
In memory of Jerry

By: Ronald D. Isaac, HM3, Echo Company 2nd Battalion,
4th Marines, 3rd Marine Division
November 1965